Paul Wildish has practised aikido for over 20 years. He is a senior instructor for the British Aikido Association and holds the rank of 5th Dan. He studied with Tetsuro Nariyama Sensei, 8th Dan, at the Shodokan Dojo in Osaka and currently teaches aikido at South Bank University in London.

# AIKIDO

## PAUL WILDISH

Thorsons

*An Imprint of* HarperCollins*Publishers*

Thorsons
An Imprint of HarperCollins*Publishers*
77–85 Fulham Palace Road,
Hammersmith, London W6 8JB

Published by Thorsons 1998
1 3 5 7 9 10 8 6 4 2

A catalogue record for this book
is available from the British Library

Text illustrations by Peter Cox

ISBN 0 7225 3588 0

Printed and bound in Great Britain by
Caledonian International Book Manufacturing Ltd, Glasgow

# CONTENTS

# INTRODUCTION

**A**ikido is a modern Japanese martial art that owes its form and inspiration to one man, Morihei Ueshiba, known to aikido students worldwide as *O Sensei*, or 'great teacher'. His art is the product of a cultural phenomenon that has no equivalent in the West. This phenomenon transformed the fighting arts of the Japanese *Samurai*, from the study of how best to kill an enemy, to the study of how best to kill the 'self'. Identifying the ego as the enemy of open selfless action, the martial arts were utilized to discipline the will and forge the spirit. Rejecting the contemplative path as 'swimming on tatami (mats)', these men believed that the only way to control violence was by understanding how to disarm it, with mind and body in harmony.

Latterly, in the 20th Century, we have seen these fighting systems converted into new kinds of sporting activities which have won popular followings across the world. No martial art has yet reached the heady heights of popularity enjoyed by football or golf, yet these unlikely cultural hybrids have reached out from their birthplace in Japan and lodged themselves firmly into our new global culture. The Japanese arts of kendo, judo and karate, together with their Chinese and Korean equivalents, can be found in every sports centre and community hall offering a bewildering choice to the potential student.

Aikido, as a clearly distinct and identifiable system of martial arts study, or *budo*, first came to international notice in the 1950s and 1960s. Slowly, it made its transfer to the West alongside its more highly profiled cousins, judo and karate. Unlike judo and karate, which have wholeheartedly opted for the international sporting model, aikido has largely rejected competitions and contests. Instead, aikido has remained committed to the idea that self-discovery and self-development are incompatible with the whole concept of winning and losing.

There are no losers in aikido, for there are no contests. Aikido is a martial art that seeks to redirect and control aggression by the art of not opposing it. It does not seek to defeat or humiliate an opponent, or even to establish competitive superiority, but only to protect.

Although its central aim is to provide a way or path to follow that will help you overcome crisis, stress and discord in both your personal and public life, it is still a very effective martial art. Aikido will equip you to deal with opponents who may be armed or unarmed, act alone, or in a gang.

Aikido's technical inheritance is derived from *Daito-ryu Aiki-jutsu*, one of the many schools of unarmed and lightly armed systems of self-defence known collectively as *jujutsu;* flexible or pliable arts. These self-defence arts share many common characteristics. They all involve unbalancing and controlling an opponent by an intelligent combination of timing, manoeuvre and the subtle manipulation of body and limbs. The techniques are broadly divided into joint twisting (wrist, elbow, shoulder) and striking *(atemi waza)* at vital points of the body. Although they can be dangerous, in aikido the principle purpose is to seize and control an opponent at the moment of contact allowing no opportunity for counter-attack.

Since the death in 1969 of aikido's founder, Morihei Ueshiba, his art has developed into a world wide movement. Different

schools and associations emphasize different facets and interpretations of his teachings. It is the purpose of this book to
present the principles that underpin the study of aikido and
examine the work of leading disciples who have modified these
principles to create some of the new forms of aikido that are
practised today.

This book is not intended to serve as an instruction manual.
Descriptions of actual techniques and their application have
been included only where they illustrate the aikido principles
discussed. The essence of aikido is in the ability to blend and
harmonise with an opponent, and can only be practised satisfactorily with a partner. This makes aikido, of all the martial
arts, a very gregarious people orientated activity where the ability to learn cooperatively is crucial.

A book of this length cannot expect to explain every aspect of
aikido's philosophy or development. I have made a selection of
the principles and practices that I feel illuminate the philosophical case for aikido and best describe its rich and varied character. I hope the reader will appreciate from reading this book that
*aikido* is not 'just another martial art', but a path that seeks
to bring out the best in the human spirit and to defend it.

# MORIHEI UESHIBA AND THE BIRTH OF AIKIDO: THE TRUE NATURE OF BUDO REVEALED

A t the turn of the 19th Century, Japan was locked into a time of sweeping social, political and economic change.

In one sudden lurch, the old *Samurai* military aristocracy under the absolute rule of the *Shogun* was brought down and the puppet Emperor freed from isolation in his Kyoto palace. He was thus restored to power as a constitutional monarch on a par with his European counterparts. This new era was named after the new monarch, the Emperor Meiji, and Japan began to claw its way into the future to take its place as an industrial and military power on an equal footing with the West.

## THE YOUNG UESHIBA

Against this backdrop Morihei Ueshiba was born on the 14th December, 1883. His was a well to do land-owning family that also owned shell-fishing rights on the bay near Tanabe, their home town in Kii Province. Now called Wakayama Prefecture, it lies on Japan's eastern Pacific seaboard. His parents Yoroku and Yuki Ueshiba, were always worried by his persistent tendency for ill health. Despite, or because of, this inherent weakness, Ueshiba was to drive himself physically all his life and in later years was noted for his strength and stamina. The Ueshiba

family were to have no more boy children. His birth was followed by that of another sister, so all the hopes and desires for the future of the family were focused, in the nature of the times, on Morihei.

In his early years he lived a robust country life dictated by the seasons and the patterns of agriculture and settlement that had changed little in centuries. Old enough to make a living for himself, he went to Tokyo in 1901 to try his luck in business, but a merchant career was not what he was looking for. Illness, this time *beriberi*, once again brought him low. However, during his short time in Tokyo he made his first serious encounter with the martial arts when he began to learn *jujutsu* (a generic name for unarmed and lightly armed Japanese self-defence techniques), under Tokusaburo Tozawa, a prominent teacher of the *Tenjin Shin'yo Ryu Jujutsu*.

## THE EXPERIENCE OF WAR

Returning to Tanabe with his health restored, he married Hatsu Itogawa, his life-long companion, in October 1902. A comfortable married life was not to be his destiny, for all the signs were pointing at war between Russia and Japan. He entered the army and was sent to Manchuria in 1905 to serve the might of the new Imperial Japan, then giving the Russians a serious pounding at Port Arthur. During his time in the army, whenever he was at his base camp for Reserves near Osaka, he renewed his martial arts training. He studied with Masakatsu Naka of the *Goto-Ha Yagyu Shingan Ryu*, a school of *jujutsu*, sword and spear arts, until he was discharged around 1908.

His return from the Russo Japanese War and service in the army left him restless and with no clear vision of his future. A lack of available space and land meant that many of Tanabe's expanding population were migrating across the Pacific to the

USA, while others sought a new start in the challenging mountain vastness of Japan's northern island, Hokkaido.

## TO HOKKAIDO AND
## JAPAN'S 'WILD WEST'

Hokkaido was Japan's 'Wild West' and much of the country was unsettled and uncultivated, having only been finally wrested from its indigenous people, the *Ainu*, in recent memory. Fired with enthusiasm and with backing from his father, he went to Hokkaido and scouted for a suitable spot where he could settle and farm. He found what he was looking for, and together with a group of other interested pioneers from his home district, he led them to found a new settlement in Shirataki, Hokkaido, in 1912.

Although fertile, Shirataki was a hostile environment with icy winters, buffeted by blizzards, deep in the heart of Hokkaido. For three years the settlers fought harsh conditions to earn a living from the earth. Eventually the introduction of lumbering, mint and pig farming at Ueshiba's inspiration brought a steady growth of income and the settlement began to function increasingly as a cohesive village community. Ueshiba, like his father before him in their home town of Tanabe, served on the village council and tended to local affairs. Undoubtedly, this period was to have a profound effect on the cast of his whole life. It gave him a deep love of nature and a passionate belief in the virtues of farming, which he was to return to at significant periods of his life. Here also in Hokkaido, he met a man of formidable reputation both for his skills and furious temper, Sokaku Takeda (1860–1943), arguably the greatest martial artist of his age.

# TAKEDA'S DISCIPLE

Ueshiba became an enthusiastic and devoted follower of Takeda, dedicating much of his time, energy and financial resources into learning new skills in *jujutsu*. He accompanied Takeda on teaching tours and generally, wherever necessary or possible, tended to his needs.

Takeda had arrived in Hokkaido in 1910 and it was to remain his base until 1930. He was a martial artist of the old school, believing in the virtues of training for practical fighting ability and the maintenance of a high state of physical alert against attack. Takeda was a man who allowed no openings and kept a constant vigilance, even requiring his students to taste food before him, lest it be poisoned. In Hokkaido, Takeda made a living as an instructor of *jujutsu* to over-stretched police departments which were struggling against the criminal gangs and bandits that took advantage of Hokkaido's frontier conditions at that time.

Takeda had learnt the *oshiki-uchi* techniques of the *Aizu* clan from Tanomo Saigo. Using the considerable experience he had gathered from the mastery of other *jujutsu* systems and schools of swordsmanship, he modified and adapted these sophisticated *jujutsu* techniques, to create what he called *Daito Ryu Aiki Jujutsu*.

Controversy within the aikido community still surrounds the question to what extent and in what detail modern aikido owes its technical foundation to *Daito Ryu*. However, recent research into the roots of aikido's early development by Stanley Pranin, editor-in-chief of the *Aikido Journal*, offers convincing proof of this legacy. Clearly Ueshiba found in *Daito Ryu* the framework upon which he was able to build a new system of *budo*, a martial art for the 20th century and beyond.

Fate, in the form of illness, once again intervened in Ueshiba's life, this time when he received a summons from his family to return to Tanabe, where his ailing father was close to death. Ueshiba immediately set out, leaving his teacher and family behind, on the long and difficult journey home to visit his father for the last time. Inexplicably, he stopped off at the religious centre of Ayabe, to offer prayers for his father and seek spiritual comfort from the leader of the *Omoto-kyo* sect, the Reverend Onisburo Deguchi.

The *Omoto-kyo* was a dynamic proselytizing sect, and part of the burgeoning *Shin* (New) *Shinto* faiths. The *Omoto-kyo* offered a heady mixture of traditional Shinto belief about the spiritual values inherent in nature and personal purification, Buddhist concepts of meditation, visualization and realization of the self, with Christian influenced ideas of revelation.

We do not know what exactly was in Ueshiba's mind or what drove him to divert from his journey to visit Deguchi, but we do know that he was deeply impressed by the man and his teaching, so much so that it was to alter the course of his life. After a short stay in Ayabe, he finally pressed on to Tanabe, to find his father already dead, which affected him greatly. After attending to arrangements and making his peace with his family for his absence at the critical time, he returned to Hokkaido. There, dividing up his possessions and leaving his house behind him as a gift to Takeda, he resolved to uproot his life once again, this time to settle at Deguchi's religious centre of Ayabe.

# THE 'NEW' FAITH

This move was a characteristically bold one, and carried unknown risks for his family. For the *Omoto-kyo*, locked by its nature outside the official religious state sponsored Shinto faith with its emphasis on loyalty to family, nation and the person of the Emperor, was regarded as subversive and its followers constantly watched by police agents. Ueshiba arrived in Ayabe early in 1920 and under Deguchi's benign patronage began one of the most creative periods of his life.

In Deguchi's teachings Ueshiba found what he was looking for; a spiritual base with which he could underpin the principles of his daily life and endeavours and more importantly guide his practice of the martial arts. As ever, enthusiastic and committed, Ueshiba sank himself into the pursuit of total awakening, through meditation and the use of powerful resonant chants based on the *kototama* ('sound spirit') religious theory, taught by the *Omoto-kyo*.

Deguchi also believed in the power of art as a religious and transforming experience, a tenet of the *Omoto-kyo* today. He encouraged his followers to take up poetry, singing, calligraphy, pottery or weaving; indeed any art where the creative and spiritual needs of mankind can be met. Deguchi recognised Ueshiba's deep spiritual qualities and his commitment to the martial arts which he did all within his power to foster. Soon, with Deguchi's support, he opened a *dojo*, or practise hall, and threw open its doors to members of the *Omoto-kyo*. There, he began to pass on the *Daito Ryu Aiki Jujutsu* he had been taught by Sokaku Takeda, who still lived in Hokkaido.

Ueshiba's relationship with Deguchi, although fundamental to aikido's spiritual foundation, was nevertheless problematic. Deguchi, who saw himself as *Miroku Buddha*, (The Buddha Who Is To Come) embroiled Ueshiba, as bodyguard and active supporter, in an ill conceived and abortive attempt to found the 'Peaceable Kingdom of the New Jerusalem' in Mongolia. Deguchi's idealistic motives accepted, he managed nevertheless to associate himself and his party in Manchuria with some dubious elements. His 'army' consisted of 130 bandits under the leadership of a man named Lu and his associate, a gunrunner, spy and probable *agent provocateur*, named Yano.

The enterprise met with utter misfortune. The Chinese authorities captured the whole party, executing Lu and his bandit 'army' and came perilously close to executing Deguchi and his small band of *Omoto-kyo* followers, including Ueshiba. A last minute reprieve delivered them into the hands of the Japanese Consul and they were repatriated to Japan, where Deguchi was promptly arrested for violation of a previous parole.

From this time on, although he maintained a deep personal devotion to his *Omoto-kyo* faith, he began to distance himself publicly from Deguchi and the sect's leadership. In this he was supported by Deguchi himself, who had determined that Ueshiba's great work would be to 'reveal the true meaning of *budo* to the world'. This period also marked the beginning of a gradual loosening of his ties to his teacher, Sokaku Takeda, who had last visited him in Ayabe for a few months at the end of April 1922. Takeda taught at Ueshiba's *dojo* and it was during these months that Takeda gave Ueshiba his full teaching licence in *Daito Ryu Aiki Jujutsu*. Deguchi and Takeda had not liked each other. Takeda regarded Deguchi as something of a

charlatan and the *Omoto-kyo* faith as contemptuous, while Deguchi saw Takeda as a man reeking of 'blood and violence'.

## THE 'STRONG' MAN OF AYABE

During his time in Ayabe, Ueshiba had built a reputation as a formidable martial artist and gifted teacher. No one seemed able, whatever their own level of skill, to stand against him, and stories of his power spread. This often led him to meet challenges, still the custom at the time, from visiting martial artists of all styles who came to test their own skills against his reputed prowess.

On one occasion in 1925, he was visited by a naval officer, renowned for his skills in kendo, Japanese fencing. In discussion about the nature of the martial arts a disagreement arose and Ueshiba challenged the officer to attempt to strike him down with a wooden sword. This the naval officer set about to do with relish. But wherever he struck and however fast, Ueshiba always managed to evade him effortlessly. When the officer finally admitted defeat and sank to the floor of the *dojo* exhausted, Ueshiba went out into the garden.

As he walked in the garden he felt the ground tremble and his body 'suffused with light'. He said later,

'I saw the divine and attained an enlightenment that was true, self-conquering, swift and sure. All at once I understood the nature of creation: the way of a warrior is to manifest divine love, a spirit that embraces and nurtures all things. Tears of gratitude and joy streamed down my cheeks. I saw the entire universe as my home, and the sun, moon, and stars as my intimate friends. All attachment to things material vanished.'

From this point forward, Ueshiba's powers seemed to increase in intensity and performance, a fact not lost on his admirers and sponsors. Prominent among his influential supporters was Admiral Takeshita, who persuaded him to disengage from his life and work in Ayabe and move to Tokyo and teach there.

Ueshiba began describing his interpretation of *Aiki Jujutsu* as *Ueshiba Ryu* or *Aiki Budo*. This marked a break from Takeda and *Daito Ryu*'s emphasis on practical considerations of self defence, to focus on the quest for a spiritual depth to his *budo*.

## TEACHER TO THE NATION'S ELITE

With Admiral Takeshita's assistance he moved to Tokyo and between 1927 and 1931 began teaching in a number of temporary *dojo*, often founded by friends and supporters. Soon he found himself *jujutsu* teacher to the nation's elite as well known military leaders and Japanese politicians became his students. This was fortunate for Ueshiba, as his association with *Omoto-kyo*, which was by then being relentlessly persecuted by the government, put him at risk of arrest. However, his friends kept him from harm and found him work teaching in military and police academies supported by a generous government stipend.

## THE RESPECT OF HIS PEERS

In October 1930, he was visited by Jigoro Kano, still regarded as the greatest innovator in the history of the Japanese martial arts. It was Kano who had taken elements of *jujutsu* techniques and located them within a system of physical education and competitive sport. The fruit of his efforts, *Kodokan Judo*, now enjoys a pre-eminent place in modern Japan's martial arts culture.

Kano, the great synthesiser of Japanese martial traditions, was drawn to see for himself what this little man, not much over 5 feet, with a legendary reputation, had to offer. Kano was suitably impressed. After witnessing a demonstration by the fiery Ueshiba, he asked that some of his own students be taken under Ueshiba's tutelage, so that Kano's *Kodokan*, then the most prestigious judo school in Japan, could have the benefit of his skills. This was an unprecedented honour and a generous acknowledgement of the quality of Ueshiba's skill and insight. For the relationship between teacher and student is a jealous one with much rivalry between the different schools of martial arts. Kano's vision was to incorporate the best of all Japanese martial arts into one school, with many facets, which could become a force for social and cultural good. In this quest he hoped to incorporate within his *Kodokan Judo* much of what Ueshiba had to offer. An agreement was reached between the two men and from that point on many famous research students from Kano's *Kodokan*, were to be found in Ueshiba's classes.

In 1931, a permanent *dojo* with living accommodation was built for Ueshiba in the Wakamatsu-cho district of Tokyo. What followed was to be steady growth of the influence and prestige of Ueshiba's *dojo*, named the *Kobukan*, or the 'Hall of Majestic Martial Virtue'. From his new headquarters, he now began to take live-in students, or *uchi-deshi*, who lived in the *dojo* or in accommodation nearby and trained on a daily basis with Ueshiba.

## THE UCHI-DESHI EXPERIENCE

The *uchi-deshi* experience has no exact parallels in the West, but it might be usefully compared to the mediaeval model of master and apprentice, where young boys were taken in and lived with the master's family, while learning the craft. The relationship had obligations on both sides. The master's were to see to his apprentice's minimum needs, to look after his health and moral welfare and pass on, to the best of his ability, the innermost principles of the craft. In return, the apprentice is obedient, diligent, loyal and performs any task assigned to him, be it menial or dignified, with equal zest and will. In most respects, the *uchi-deshi*'s experience closely models that of the Western mediaeval apprentice, described above. However there are important differences in the relationship of the *sensei* (teacher) and *uchi-deshi*, that are more akin to that of a religious teacher and his disciples.

The young men who had come to study with Ueshiba had heard of his amazing skills and had come to live a life of small reward and great hardship. This was a disciplined world where they must rise early, wash and scrub *dojo* and quarters, attend to their *sensei*'s needs, and all before early practice! For an aikido *uchi-deshi*, that was also a testing endeavour, for we have a picture drawn by his students of a man of genius and singular purpose, with all the contradictions, passions and strains that such qualities put upon relationships with others. The picture we have of these times is of a strict and severe teacher who could fly into a great rage when an *uchi-deshi* failed to understand, but in the next moment could dissolve into mischievous laughter as if having a private joke with the gods. We do know that many of that small but significant band of young men, and a few women, who spent months or years training personally with Ueshiba, went on to become creative teachers in their own right and were so imprinted by the experience that they thought with an 'aikido-mind'.

So valued is this experience in the psychology of aikido that many thousands of young men and women, increasingly from outside of Japan, trek to the *dojos* of Ueshiba's successors and

disciples, in the desire to profit by that deeply traditional and close personal bonding that is the *deshi* experience to this day. It is valued because it teaches persistence, determination and effort. The expectations of the *sensei* are high but realistic and the lessons to be learned are more about humility, cooperation and integrity than they are about skill. When Ueshiba took in a student he was forging the character of aikido into his or her mind. This led him to pick his students with care, only those who came with impeccable credentials would be let through the door.

His method of teaching was also problematic, for he taught intuitively to no agreed programme or structure. He followed his own course of discovery in the expectation that learning would spring up behind him. This intuitive method was central to the traditions of classical *budo* schools, from which he drew his own inspiration and precedent. But it was in great contrast to Kano and his judo. Where Kano was concerned to explain how techniques worked according to their mechanics and the judo principles that lay within them, Ueshiba enjoined his students to learn naturally. The practical expression of this method was for Ueshiba to demonstrate his techniques, then invite his students to reproduce them without benefit of explanation. Only after a long apprenticeship of being on the receiving end, taking endless falls and being subjected to the fiercest joint-locks, would they be allowed to perform these techniques themselves.

This never seemed to put off the small, but highly select and influential number of recruits that continually replenished his devoted following. War and conquest in China and Manchuria kept his skills in demand from the military and police, and Ueshiba made many trips to areas occupied by the Japanese forces to teach officers and intelligence units. At the outbreak of war with the USA in 1941, testimony from his students suggests that he was becoming increasingly disturbed and saddened by the arrogance and brutality of Japan's Imperial forces. In 1942, he resigned all his teaching commitments and retired to Iwama, in the countryside, about two hours train ride from Tokyo.

## RETREAT TO IWAMA

Ueshiba had been buying land in Iwama since 1938, and now with his wife, moved again to settle in a modest dwelling to farm and practice *budo*, away from the fierce contest raging across the world. Sickness beset him, but he was determined once again to find the strength to teach the message of 'true *budo*'; that it protects and preserves, eschews gratuitous violence and is the model for an 'Art of Peace'. In Iwama the final transition from *jujutsu* to aikido was made.

With Japan's defeat at the hands of the Allies, the conditions for all martial arts was initially bleak. The Allied Powers regarded the martial arts schools with suspicion and in many cases justifiably regarded them as breeding grounds for militarist ideology, incompatible with the new democratic Japan they were busy establishing. All martial arts practice was initially banned and Western sports encouraged. Those that still held to a belief in the positive social value of the martial arts began to regroup, practise in secret and rethink the future of *budo*.

Naturally judo, which had already incorporated sentiments about popular participation in sport and physical education, was in the forefront of presenting a new acceptable face to the Allied authorities. Aikido was also making an effort to recast its message in new ways and forms, carried forward by the inspiration of Ueshiba's only surviving son Kisshomaru, and senior students who gathered in Tokyo.

# THE POST-WAR YEARS

Aikido went through a thin period after the war. The old *dojo* in Tokyo had been occupied by squatters, and war meant many missing faces among its ranks. By the end of the 1950s, with the ban lifted, martial arts were on the move again. Through the efforts of Kisshomaru Ueshiba and others, the *Kobukan* had become the *Aikikai Foundation Hombu* (the Aikikai headquarters school) and was actively teaching classes again, to an even wider audience. Crucially in September 1955, Kisshomaru persuaded his father to give a public demonstration of aikido at a large Tokyo department store. This was a significant break with tradition. Many masters such a the great swordsman Hakudo Nakayama practised their special techniques in seclusion and away from prying eyes. Ueshiba stepped out from behind his *dojo* doors and amazed those who came to see his ability to overpower and subdue multiple attackers, armed and unarmed; the calm centre within the maelstrom.

# AIKIDO REACHES OUT

Aikido began to gain a popular audience in Japan and a place in the universities, while through the efforts of early pioneers it found a footing in France, Hawaii, the USA and the UK. In 1961 this expansion was celebrated with a visit by Ueshiba to Hawaii, to open the Honolulu *Aikikai dojo*, where aikido had found fertile root.

In his later years his presence as a spiritual force increased, no less than in the way he looked with a flowing white beard, bright, sometimes fierce eyes, wearing traditional white *hakama*, (divided skirt-like trousers) and *dogi*, (training jacket). When he visited the *dojo* in Tokyo from his retreat in Iwama, he commanded undivided attention despite the difficulties his loyal students had in understanding the long lectures he gave on *aiki*, and his *Omoto-kyo* inspired theology.

In Iwama he continued to study, farm and practise aikido. He prayed daily at the *Aiki* Shrine he had built in the early 1960s, in front of an earlier, smaller structure erected in 1948, until increasing frailty made it necessary for him to spend more time in Tokyo. Despite his age, he kept teaching until February of 1969 when he was admitted to Keio University Hospital, for treatment for liver cancer. With little more that could be done he was released into the care of his family and died on 26 April 1969, aged eighty-six.

From a small *dojo* in Ayabe, aikido has grown into an essentially non-competitive martial way, practised worldwide. His students and their successors continue to pass on his message with different emphases and methodologies, but all in the spirit of Ueshiba's vision; that it should be about the avoidance of conflict and the preservation of harmony.

# THE WAY OF HARMONY: AI KI DO: THE WAY OF HARMONY WITH THE SPIRIT

**W**hen Morihei Ueshiba chose the name *ai ki do* (or the 'Way (*do*) of Harmony (*ai*) with the Spirit (*ki*)') for his new interpretation of *aiki jujutsu* techniques, he was marking an important contrast of principle between his Way and those of previous classical martial forms. Classical *jujutsu* understood attack and defence as *kobo-itchi*, or a unified initiative, which cannot be separated in action. Ueshiba *Sensei* based his aikido on the principle of *go no sen*, which is an entirely defensive initiative. *Go no sen* has many complexities, but it may be seen as the defender making no first move or response to threat of attack, until that attack has been launched. The initiative of *go no sen* is formed by the defender's ability to read the intention of danger in an opponent's posture or 'mind', and to be so tuned that the response comes almost simultaneously with the launch of any attack. This obviously takes many years of training and 'tuning' to master satisfactorily, but to an *aikidoka* (a student of aikido), it is a practical register of how far along the way he or she has come towards developing an open heart and mind.

The *aikidoka* trains to respond to threats and dangers from an ethical position that accords with that basic human instinct of fair play and a refusal to initiate violence or inflict unnecessary suffering. To do this, the *aikidoka* trains in the techniques of aikido, based on this principle of *go no sen*, to improve the quality of his skill. This is not in the vain pursuit of personal prowess, but a responsibility to acquire sufficient skill to neutralize an aggressor with the minimum physical effort and to leave that aggressor chastened, but unhurt. Although all modern martial ways hold to an ethic of self-defence and a refusal to 'cast the first stone', few could claim that their block, kicks, punches, locks or throws leave no damage in their wake. In this way aikido lays claim to be unique.

## THE OBJECT OF AIKIDO

The object of aikido is to be able to:

- Perceive a threat.
- Respond instinctively (but humanely) to an aggressive act.
- Redirect and neutralize the physical force of that attack.
- Leave both the defender and the attacker unharmed.

This principle is pursued in the *dojo* (training hall) not merely to understand the technical nature of the art, or its cultural integrity, but for the lessons we may draw upon in life outside the *dojo*. The quest of the *aikidoka* is to tune the mind and the body so that they unite harmoniously and to equip the individual to react spontaneously and appropriately to all situations, at home, at work, in study or at play.

We may see how that can be done by examining the meaning of the *kanji* (Japanese ideogrammatic script), for each of the three characters that form the name, or rather the concept of *ai ki do*.

# AI: HARMONY WITH ALL THINGS

*Ai*, as we have seen, is often translated as 'harmony' or 'affinity', and can be understood as an individual's ability to adapt quickly to the changing circumstances encountered in life. Therefore it models a social purpose which aikido seeks to reflect as:

- The development of a healthy mind and body.
- The promotion of a decency and robustness of the spirit.
- The ability to live in harmony with your *self* and *all* around you.

In this Ueshiba was declaring a moral philosophy for his teachings which sees man and nature as a union; an inseparable alliance. To understand nature is therefore to understand man. Aikido seeks to bring about this understanding by implanting within its practice the principle of circularity, evident in the movements of matter within the universe itself. Thus there are no straight lines in aikido and force is never opposed with force. Instead, the aikido practitioner circles around, alongside or behind an opponent to blend with their force and lead them to a safe and benevolent solution. Ueshiba's aikido enjoins us to be benevolent, not only to our self or our opponent, but to all things, serving nature through both our moral and physical actions.

This open benevolence of mind requires flexibility of thought and attitude which the *aikidoka* trains to reflect in bodily actions. The actions of the body as learned and demonstrated in aikido practice become a means for developing that open, human-hearted spirit, which is represented by the character *ai*.

In a very practical self-defence sense, this flexibility of mind and body are about perception and the ability to read the intentions of an opponent and deal with them instinctively. The *aikidoka* trains to reduce the time between perceiving a threat, the decision to act against that threat, and the form of action taken.

# KI: TAPPING THE LIFE FORCE

## WHAT IS KI?

*Ki* has become a more familiar concept in the West, since aikido was first introduced. The popularity of Chinese medicine, acupuncture, *tai chi* and alternative therapies with Japanese origins such as *shiatsu* and *reiki*, have made the concept of *ki*, or in its Chinese rendition *chi*, almost commonplace. Here *ki*, which aikido translates as 'spirit', can also be understood as 'vitality', 'energy', or even 'breath'. It is the natural movement of this unseen force through the body, that encourages and sustains our health and well-being.

## WHAT IS THE POINT OF KI?

Within these healing systems *ki* is seen as the cosmic life-force, immanent in all things, animating life and the movement of the universe. The flow of *ki* through the channels of vitality within and without us is the source of energy and strength upon which aikido draws. Being able to tap into this power, control it and use it, not only gives us the ability to heal ourselves and others, but to use its power to heal aggression and counter violence. For the *aikidoka* the development of this understanding and ability to 'summon *ki*' is the measure of both his physical and spiritual progress in the art.

## HOW DO WE DEVELOP KI?

The development of an awareness of *ki* and how it can be tapped is therefore an essential aspect of aikido training. This training is physical, part of the fabric and structure of aikido technique and requires no blind acceptance of belief by the student. The proof that *ki* is a force that can be recognised and used, is left to time and the student's progress in training, which is designed to bring awareness of the elements of *ki*, that are outlined below.

# THE TANDEN OR HARA

In Eastern thought, the psycho-physical centre of the body where *ki* is understood to be focused, is situated in the *tanden* or *hara*. This is often termed the 'one point' and is located approximately two inches below the navel; corresponding approximately to the body's centre of gravity. By concentrating on this point and keeping our balance low and centred, we learn to use our whole body as one without reliance on the strength of our upper torso, or any one set of powerful limbs. Indeed we increase the power of torso, arms and legs by maintaining this centre of gravity.

It is also the place where the breath power of the body can be encouraged by deep abdominal breathing through a variety of exercises, so that we learn to use the full capacity of our lungs in training and in life.

## CHUSHIN: CENTRAL ALIGNMENT

Our ability to be aware of our *tanden* also allows us to maintain the central alignment of the body. Rarely do we sit or walk erect in a central alignment and so we are prevented from using the full power of our hips or breath. Aikido seeks through its training methods to correct this misalignment, by developing a good posture or *kamae*. This requires the hips to lead the body, keeping our torso erect and our arm movements originating from this centre line. As the body is centred so is the mind, focusing forward to command the energy of the whole body at the instant required.

## KOKYU RYOKU: BREATH POWER

Breath is part of the rhythm of life, oxygenating our blood and fuelling body and mind. Practices that encourage good, deep breathing to develop the capacity of the lungs are important for all physical pursuits, be it dance, athletics, yoga or a martial art.

In aikido, *kokyu* is the channel along which *ki* flows. Students are taught to draw breath deep down into the abdomen and to utilise its power by exhaling powerfully from the *tanden* when performing a technique.

This breath power must become natural and instinctive; it should not be a conscious mechanical act that will distract our senses and hamper our concentration. Neither must we allow fear or panic to hamper our breath and reduce our ability to take effective action. Instead we must keep a calm, relaxed mind, or centre, that is able to regulate the rhythm of our breathing to meet all situations appropriately. By diligent practice in the development of breath power, the aikido student learns to breath freely and rhythmically throughout the course of the most stressful physical or emotional circumstances.

*Kokyu* is also the conjunction of your breathing with that of an opponent. It allows you to time and control the tempo of your breathing and the reflexes of your body to arrive exactly in that place and moment when decisive action to neutralize your opponent is required.

To summarize, the aikidoka must be able to:

- Operate with a calm, open mind that has no expectations and makes no prejudgements about courses of action.
- Be alert to the 'one point' where the body's centre of gravity is located.
- Maintain the central alignment and balance of the body.
- Breath deeply and naturally.

Only when these elements are integrated into the student's body and mind can it be said that they are able to use their *ki* effectively.

# DO: A PATH TO UNDERSTANDING

*Do* is the word used in Japan to describe a Way, or path (*michi*) to understanding and self-realization. It is understood from the outset that there is no end to this path. It is a lifetime's journey. For even the enlightened mind is continually challenged by daily events. There is no once and for all time perfect state to reach in this life. It follows that this lifetime's journey, carries with it a commitment not required ordinarily by Western concepts of sport.

*Do* is both a physical activity and a cultural endeavour that seeks a spiritual outcome in the cultivation of mind, body and spirit for the benefit of both the individual and society, in order to make better people and consequently, a better world. This commitment is very different from that required of the Western sportsman, who plays the game for the joy and competitiveness of it, where a winning performance is all and the manner of that performance secondary. In a *do* form, the manner of the performance is by far the most important element of a student's learning, for it will be through the manners of performance that character and spiritual insight manifest themselves.

All modern martial Ways, or *budo*, place great emphasis therefore on the manners of performance, as expressed in the concept of *reigi-saho*. This can simply, but incompletely, be translated as etiquette or civil manners. The forms of conduct which constitute *reigi-saho* are there to be followed at the beginning, during and at the end of training. They start as soon as you enter the *dojo* and must be observed until you leave it, with the aim of becoming integrated into your character and thereby informing your conduct in everyday life. These rules and procedures of behaviour emphasize courtesy, humility, mutual support, the duty of care, and most importantly, respect. There is respect for the traditions, teachings, spiritual and physical practice of the Way; respect for your teachers, fellow students and others; and finally a profound self-respect, that comes with no conceit or ego to it.

The *do*, or Way is therefore the counter-point of *jutsu*, an art or skill, which is learnt essentially for its practical application and effectiveness. This is not to say that a *do* form, as in *aikido*, puts no premium on the standard of performance or the practical effectiveness of technique. Good technique obviously demonstrates a discipline, commitment to training and profound understanding of the Way on the part of the *aikidoka*. However, in any activity we do not all share the same advantages or expectations, flair or ability and we may never be the sportsman, painter, potter or calligrapher we dreamed of being. The Way recognises these differences in skill and natural ability but sees the pursuit of skill for its own sake as an empty exercise. The point is not the perfection of that skill alone, but the sincerity with which it is sought and the insight gained.

## WHAT THEN IS AIKIDO?

When *ai* and *ki* are joined to form *aiki*, we then have a state that we can describe as an alert, imperturbable mind, with no evil intentions or fear. This state is mirrored in the 'open', reflexive and relaxed posture, or *kamae*, adopted by the *aikidoka* and is the objective of all training. The primary purpose of aikido is therefore to promote the individual's ability to call on this the state of *aiki*, not only when faced with the physical threat of assault but in every area of conflict and challenge experienced in life. Through the learning of technique and its perfection, the *aikidoka* is given physical challenges which can only be resolved when body and mind act together, in perfect concert. Through the practice of aikido, what the body learns will teach and refine the mind, encouraging the student to avoid conflict and confrontation. True strength and assertiveness is witnessed by

the ability to control and command the mind and lead others from contest to collaboration.

The Way of *aiki*, cannot be easily equated with the taking up of a sport or hobby, although one's initial motivation for beginning aikido may have the same honest impulse. Aikido is a discipline for the mind and the body, that recognises no distinction between them. The mind is the body and the body is the mind – train both and you forge the human spirit.

This may make aikido sound like religion, too heavy on discipline and no fun. This is its exact antithesis, for aikido seeks to be inclusive and does not lay down dogma or prescriptions to restrict or exclude. Because its techniques are fluid, evolving and reinventing themselves with every circumstance, the individual is offered a very personal creative expression of the Way, related to their character and their physical circumstances. Laughter and the sheer joy of commanding the body to move and flow in harmony with others is as important to aikido as it is to dance, with which its flowing, circular patterns of movement are often compared.

Aikido is experienced through practice with a partner. Indeed, very little can be done on your own. As the techniques have their dangers and limits, bonds of confidence and trust must be built between students to foster a positive community of learning. In this Neo-Confucian model of learning each student is required to assist and progress the learning of others through the shared effort of partner practice. Each in turn acts as attacker or defender and each in turn is thrown or controlled by wrist or elbow lock. Trust is fundamental to the practice of aikido and 'over enthusiastic' or spiteful application of techniques is easily spotted and finds no toleration in the *dojo*. The codes of etiquette that constitute aikido *reigi-saho*, embody these principles of trust and mutual respect and serve to remind the individual of the compact with the Way that they have made.

Aikido can be approached on many fronts. At the simplest level it offers an interesting and creative activity designed to build the body's strength, flexibility and the energy to help sustain a healthy life. It offers a very practical and effective method of self-defence, suitable for men, women and children, irrespective of shape, size or strength. The confidence to defend oneself, without resort to unnecessary or gratuitous escalation of violence, is both an important personal and also a civil confidence in our modern world. Aikido also provides a spiritual path for those who seek it. This is implicit rather than explicit in its practice and is for the individual to discover as it is revealed through experience in the *dojo*. The individual can approach aikido through any or all of these fronts, with each characteristic or aspect having more importance at one time than another. Aikido lays down a path and offers the guidance of teachers and fellow *aikidoka* to point the Way.

# FIRST STEPS IN THE DOJO: THE 'BEGINNER'S MIND'

**A**ikido is imbued with an idealistic and humane philosophy that wishes to promote a more peaceful and harmonious world, by disciplining the conduct and spirit of men and women to avoid conflict and bring reconciliation. In the tradition of the *Zen* influenced Japanese arts and ways, it sets out to accomplish this aim by dedication to a physical pursuit that is both aesthetic, practical, and united in the search for perfect form. This 'perfect form' is not sought for its own sake but for the challenge to our learning it represents. Through our quest for this form, the spiritual and human lessons are drawn and our discipline and tenacity is rewarded.

The student naturally requires guidance and a framework of action to follow. For each aspect of the practice of aikido is designed to convey social, cultural and spiritual understandings that will help us on our path along the Way. In all aikido *dojo* there will be forms of etiquette and behaviour that have been transferred from an Oriental culture whose outlook is framed by Taoist, Confucian and Buddhist philosophy. The meanings entrenched in these cultural practices are implicit rather than explicit and do not always sit easily with a Western rationalist world-view. The purpose of this chapter is to describe the practice of aikido, its forms, rituals and basic exercises and to explain their purpose and function in developing our understanding of aikido principles.

## THE BEGINNER'S MIND

'You need to realise that when you practise from the state of the beginner all the way to the stage of immutable wisdom, then you must go back to the status of the beginner again.'

Takuan (*Zen* master)

One of the most important lessons to be drawn from the study of aikido, is to approach each aspect of your learning freshly, with what is known as the beginner's mind. The Zen master Takuan, explained this concept through the analogy of martial arts practice in this way. At first the beginner understands nothing of technique or defensive positioning, therefore his mind is not fixed on a particular way of responding to an attack. When the attack comes, the response is spontaneous and instinctive.

Later, when the student is further down the path of learning, the right body position or the placing of the hand become all too important, confusing the mind and inhibiting the speed and naturalness of reactions. This is the awkward phase when there seems far too much to learn and everything seems to be happening at once. Yet if you persist and continue to practice regularly, over many days and months, the stances and techniques become ingrained and instinctive, and your response to a strike becomes as spontaneous and as unthought of as the beginner once again.

The lesson to be drawn is that we must empty our mind of distracting thoughts and attachments that will hinder us from remaining open and responsive to whatever may come our

way. Each time we are shown a technique, if we try to look with a beginner's mind, as if this is the first time we have seen it, then our chances of truly seeing how it works are increased. The educational philosophy of the martial arts attempts therefore to resolve a paradox, to implant specific skills and techniques while at the same time encouraging our natural and instinctive spontaneity through a complex process of discipline and training.

The burden of this message is that, however far along the path of learning we may be, our experience can have the same value if we come to it without the baggage of preconceptions and prejudices. For the beginner, this offers a positive message of hope. The confusion and frustration that may be felt when trying to hold on to new learning and to translate it into action, is quite normal and to be expected. Indeed the more you try to hold on to, the less you are likely to learn. Instead the beginner is encouraged to enter into a process where, through constant practice and repetition, the body will learn to be untrammelled by the mind. Through this process they will have a successful engagement with aikido.

## THE DOJO: A PLACE FOR THE TEACHING OF THE WAY

The *dojo* is a special place which has been dedicated to the purpose of teaching and practising the way. It has only become a special place because of the respect shown to it by the students of the Way, in this case aikido. That respect is only owed by them to the *dojo* because of their confidence in the Way itself. The *dojo* is after all only a hall, a room or a gymnasium. There are few dedicated aikido *dojo* in the West, or in aikido's homeland Japan, as the costs to support such institutions are comparatively high, wherever you are in the world. Full-time *dojo* do exist, either supported as the headquarters, or *hombu dojo*, of some association, or belonging to a professional instructor. It is much more likely that your first impression of a *dojo* will be a visit to an aikido class in a community hall or sports centre. However, the class will have given that space the special status of a *dojo* and it will be treated accordingly.

## THE TRADITIONAL DOJO

It may be useful to carry into the training hall with us a picture of what a traditional *dojo* looks like, and hold that in our imagination as we enter. The space should conform as much to that picture as the nature of the surroundings will allow. First we should encounter a small lobby or entrance area, from where in modern purpose built *dojo*, changing rooms would be accessible. Here a reception area would allow the opportunity to conduct the business of the *dojo*, the registering of names and collection of fees, without intruding on the training area itself. Here also, would be racks or a space for leaving one's outdoor shoes.

The etiquette observed in the aikido *dojo* is, of course, part of the fabric of Japanese cultural life and reflects the social manners both of today's Japan and of the practices of the classical *budo* schools of the Tokugawa Era (17th to 19th Centuries).

Just as one does not enter a Japanese house with shoes on, neither should you enter the *dojo* with shoes which have been worn on the street. This is the first practical, as well as symbolic act. The dust and grime of the street is not brought into the *dojo* where others will be walking in bare feet and, symbolically, you leave the outside world behind you with your shoes. It signals that you are in that other place, dedicated to the purpose of teaching aikido.

### TATAMI

Once inside the training area itself, you will find the floor of the *dojo* covered in *tatami*, or matting, providing the safety area on which the training will take place. These mats were traditionally made of straw and covered the floor areas of homes, temples and palaces alike. Today these mats are formed from dense layers of foam and rubber to give protection from falls. Their dimensions, 1m by 2m, dictate the pattern in which they are laid on the floor, usually arranged as a square or rectangular shaped area. The mats may cover the entire floor, or have a surrounding space where students may walk off the mat area.

## THE KAMIZA (UPPER SEAT)

The working orientation of the mat and the central focus of the *dojo*, is the *kamiza (joza)*, the upper or 'above' seat. On this wall the *kamidana*, a small Shinto altar or shrine arranged with offerings of flowers or fruit, may be located. Alongside the *kamiza*, will be a portrait of the founder of aikido, Morihei Ueshiba or perhaps of another prominent teacher to which the *dojo* is attached, or both. The *dojo* may also display a framed *gaku*, or brushed work of Japanese calligraphy, whose philosophical meaning the student is invited to reflect upon and use as an inspiration for training. This may be the word *ai ki do* itself brushed by a skilled calligrapher and teacher. *O Sensei*, or Great Teacher, as Morihei Ueshiba is known by *aikidoka* worldwide, was a skilled calligrapher himself and many *dojo* treasure examples of his brush work on their *kamiza* wall.

The wall on which the *kamiza* is arranged forms the *shomen*, the head of the *dojo*, beneath which the teacher or teachers sits facing the students on the opposite side of the mat or *shimoza*, lower seat. Senior students sit, in their turn, to the left of the *kamiza*, termed *joseki* (upper side), and lower grades to the right, or *shimoseki* (lower side). The *kamiza* or *shomen* forms the symbolic head or face of the *dojo* and the attention of the students is directed towards it when carrying out the opening and closing forms of ritual observance required by the *dojo*.

Traditionally, a *dojo*'s walls should not be covered with unnecessary clutter or decoration. Apart from the *kamidana*, the racks for wooden training weapons and perhaps a small *takenomo*, or alcove space, where another brush work scroll or flower arrangement may be set, no distractions are allowed to interfere with the student's concentration.

One can see that the *dojo* is both conceived as a spiritual space and one where vigorous and demanding physical exercise can take place. Therefore it is accorded a respect similar to that of a Buddhist or Shinto temple. This is a harder concept to hold on to when you are walking through a large sports hall, past basket-ball and badminton courts to get to that small corner where an aikido mat area is laid out. However, the more you are able to hold on to the idea of a special place the more respect you can give to your own training.

## REIGI-SAHO: THE ETIQUETTE OF THE HEART

As we have seen, the observance of *reigi-saho*, or forms of etiquette, are of principal importance in demonstrating the student's perception and understanding of aikido's heart and mind. The courtesies they represent extend beyond their outward physical rituals and are concerned with our social and moral conduct, not only in the *dojo* but also in the conduct of our everyday life.

*Reigi-saho*, is therefore not merely the correct observance of ritual or etiquette but the manner of our conduct, in all the circumstances thrown up by our training in aikido. The true spirit of *reigi-saho* is observed through our human qualities of modesty, respect and concern for others and the humanity that we demonstrate in the application of technique. Different *dojo*, or schools, may have variations in the observance of ritual, but all hold fast to the concept of *reigi-saho* as exemplary, compassionate, and civil behaviour, requiring the student to be alert to the needs and safety of others at all times. *Reigi-saho* is therefore an important part of our training, assisting us to win control of our mind and reminding us that we have a place within a community, and that its concern for us must be reciprocated in our actions and our thoughts.

## RITSU-REI: STANDING BOW

The first act upon entering and the last before leaving the *dojo*, or training hall, is the performance of *ritsu-rei*, or a standing bow, in the direction of the *kamiza*, or *shomen*. This is accomplished from a neutral stance *(shizen hontai)*; that is, the body straight and relaxed, with hands held palms inward and fingers slightly flexed to the side of the body and feet close together at the heels. The head and torso are then inclined 30º from the waist while the hands slide down to rest with fingertips lightly touching the front of the thighs near the knees. Your eyes should follow the movement of your body, maintaining a central alignment. Held for a moment, the head and body then return to rest in neutral posture once more. The movement should be made with as much natural grace and simple dignity as possible.

*Ritsu-rei*, is performed on many other occasions in the *dojo*, such as before stepping on or off the mat, to other *aikidoka* before engaging in practice and most importantly to your teacher when receiving guidance or instruction. This is not a religious observance or an act of servility. It must be viewed as much an act of self-respect and as an outward sign of respect to others. The bow is freely given between all *aikidoka*, with more senior *aikidoka* receiving more measured and slightly deeper bows than their juniors marking their greater experience of aikido. As such, each *aikidoka*, as they pass along the Way, will in their turn experience the approving respect of their fellow *aikidoka*. This hierarchy of respect is meritocratic,

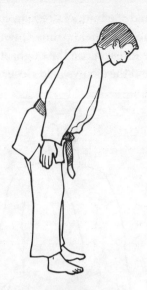

Ritsu Rei (standing bow)

but that merit is broadly judged and is open to all who persist in their aikido journey.

## SEIZA: SITTING

Before the formal rituals of the opening of a class take place, all the *aikidoka* who have lined up on the *shimoza* side of the *dojo* in order of rank or grade are called to order and required to sit in the formal position of *seiza* facing the *kamiza* or *shomen*. In this posture the *aikidoka* assumes a kneeling position generally by withdrawing the left foot a half step, then placing the left knee on the mat with the toes bent, keeping the head and back erect and the right hand resting on the raised right knee. In turn the right leg is withdrawn to form a triangle of the two knees, held apart at the distance of least two fists, with the feet closed together and the big toes folded over each other, left over the right. The back is held straight with the abdomen pressed slightly forward and the buttocks resting comfortably between your heels. The hands are held palms down and fingers together resting with the forearms on the thighs, the fingers inclining slightly inwards and the elbows held close to the body.

Seiza (sitting)

To rise, the process is undertaken in reverse by raising the hips and pausing to rest once again on bent toes, before raising first the right knee then the left to come to stand once again in *shizen hontai*, or the natural stance. The whole action should be completed in one dignified fluid movement.

*Seiza* is an important position of rest and is the required sitting position for the opening and closing rituals of the aikido session. The student is also encouraged to sit in this position when the *Sensei* has called a halt to practice, in order to teach or demonstrate some aspect of an aikido technique to the class.

Sitting in the *seiza* position can be uncomfortable for the unpractised. However when the student has developed the ability to keep this position for short or more sustained periods comfortably, it helps to develop the feeling of being grounded with body and mind centred on the *hara*. In this way *seiza* could be said to reflect the still inner heart that the aikido student struggles for.

## ZAREI: SEATED BOW

Once all are in *seiza*, the *sensei* or teacher kneeling in front of the class will manoeuvre to face towards the *kamiza*. Then, according to the ritual of the *dojo*, he will signal by clapping, in the shinto manner of calling the attention of 'those who are above', that all should make a seated bow in the direction of the *kamiza* or *shomen*. This may alternatively be signalled by the most senior *aikidoka* on the *joseki* side of the *dojo*, calling out the command 'kamiza ni rei' or 'shomen ni rei'.

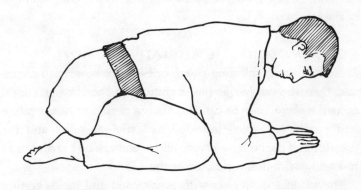

Zarei (kneeling bow)

The *zarei*, or seated bow, is executed by placing the palms of the hands on the mat, fingers inclined inwards, fore fingers touching to form a triangular shape approximately six inches in front of the knees. The upper body is again inclined to a 30° angle or more, the head in line with the trunk, towards the hands resting in position on the mat. It is important not to let the head bend independently, or allow the hips to rise when completing *zarei* and once again to maintain a fluent, unhurried dignity. The bow is held for a moment before reversing the procedure.

When the *sensei* has turned once again towards the class, another *zarei* is performed by students to teacher and teacher to students as a formal signal of mutual respect. From the students, respect is given to the teacher for his or her knowledge and experience and ability to communicate and pass on all that he or she has learned from and about aikido. From the teacher, respect is given to the students for their attentiveness, dedication and consistent willingness to learn.

At the conclusion of a class, the students will again be called upon to complete a *zarei*, in reverse order, firstly between students and teacher, then secondly together, in acknowledgement of the *kamiza*.

## MOKUSO: THE MEDITATIVE MOMENT

Preceding the concluding ritual, or between bowing to *kamiza* and then the teacher at the beginning of the class, a period named *mokuso*, may be called. This is a period of recuperation and meditative quiet, intended to settle the mind and the breathing of the body, readying one to embark on practice or to re-engage with the world outside the *dojo*.

The *aikidoka* sit in *seiza* with eyes closed and hands resting lightly on the thighs, or held palms up with the tips of the thumbs touching to form an 'O'. Relaxed abdominal breathing is undertaken and the *aikidoka* is encouraged to empty the mind and seek an open receptive consciousness by refusing to fix, or hold on to individual thoughts.

*Mokuso*, a practice which is observed in common with almost all Japanese martial ways or *budo*, has its likely origins in *zazen*, the meditation exercises of Zen Buddhism and Shinto ritual. The period is generally signalled by either the teacher or senior ranking *aikidoka* on the *joseki* side of the *dojo* calling for *mokuso*. All the students then settle in *seiza*, their backs relaxed and straight 'like a column of smoke rising on a calm day', eyes closed and breathing deeply and rhythmically. This position is maintained for a minute or two, until the command for the end of the period, *mokuso yame* is called.

It is not intended that *mokuso* should be the same in-depth meditative experience sought through *zazen*, but it is a valuable period of shifting reflection and quiet, where the heart, breath and mind can be calmed and readjusted before embarking on the next cycle of activity.

## TAISO (PHYSICAL EXERCISES)

All aikido *dojo* will include in its curriculum, as do many other sports, a short period of warming-up exercises, specifically designed to suit the physical nature of the activity. The actual routines are not formally laid down, but many *dojo* follow similar practices. All these routines are aimed at loosening and flexing the joints and gently raising the heart rate and stimulating the flow of energy, or *ki*, through the body. These exercises will be relaxed and gradual, and avoid excessively strenuous or muscle straining routines. Stretching often forms part of the routines, but the beginner will be encouraged to take everything at their own pace.

As with all sports, the best physical preparation for aikido is the practice of aikido itself. Therefore learning to move with economy and fluency and developing stamina is far more important to aikido than building an extra bank of muscles or hardening the body. To this end, aikido schools include in their

38    practice a range of basic exercises, which form the building
blocks for all aikido body positions and movements.

Fundamental to learning the art of aikido, is the development of central alignment and the ability to keep the body's centre of gravity low and the body balanced, whether still or in dynamic motion. The posture the body adopts is the key to this process. Aikido pays particular attention to teaching basic body positions (*hanmi*) and stances (*kamae*), from which all responsive actions stem.

## SHISEI (POSTURE)

Forming the basis of all posture, is *sei ritsu*, the natural standing position of everyday life. Here the feet are spaced apart, directly below the shoulders. The body is relaxed and flexible, with the back straight and the head erect. Arms are held comfortably at the sides of the body with the hands resting on the upper thighs. From this position the *aikidoka* can move easily into *hidari* (left) *kamae*, by simply moving the left foot forward a half step, pointing slightly to the outside, while the back foot turns 90º to the right. The body is held in an oblique position, torso, head and eyes facing forward, forming a stable position framed by the triangular positioning of body and feet, known as *sankakutai*. *Migi*, (right), *kamae* is entered by moving the right foot forward and is the opposite or mirror position of *hidari kamae*.

Linked to these *kamae*, is the position of the arm, which is extended to the front of the body with the elbow slightly bent and the hand held upright and centred. The edge of the hand forms *tegatana* or hand-blade, in imitation of the sword-blade. In aikido, the hand becomes the sword, with the body moving in and out of positions similar to the stances of Japanese swordsmanship in order to establish the control of defensive and operative space.

Sei ritsu (natural standing posture)

This ideal operative space for reaction and manoeuvre, is termed *ma-ai* (distance), and is defined by the space opened between two *aikidoka* facing each other in left or right posture, the edges of their hand-blades just meeting. This distance will vary according to the stance adopted. The stances are either *ai-hanmi* (mutual oblique position), when both partners face each other in half-right or half-left stance, or *gyaku-hanmi* (reverse oblique position) when they are standing half-right faced to half-left.

In this spatial relationship, it would be necessary for an aggressor to take a step forward before being able to land a blow or seize hold. Similarly, it requires one step forward for the *aiki-doka* to enter and control the defensive space of an opponent.

*Ma-ai* is of course further conditioned by the use of weapons, where the extra reach may give an attacker an advantage.

PRINCIPLES OF AIKIDO

Allowances and adjustments in the spatial relationship must naturally be made to compensate for this, but the principle remains the same. The *aikidoka* seeks by the control of *ma-ai* (distance) to keep an opponent beyond the edge of his hand-blade with his body forming the calm centre of an invisible circle of protection. Any entry into this space has the advantage of this reactive opportunity, securing a timing moment for the *aikidoka* to exploit. In this way on the instant of aggression, the *aikidoka* may choose to turn swiftly, avoiding and deflecting an attack, or enter into the opponent's space, to subdue them with a blow or joint-locking immobilization.

Posture, or *kamae*, is not only important when at rest or awaiting an attack, but is central to movement and the application of aikido technique. As we learn to stand in good posture, we must also learn to move in good posture. Aikido has a particular pattern of moving the feet, designed to give a stable base from which to act in any eventuality. If the student is to act with a calm and centred mind, she must also learn to move so that her centre follows the movement of her feet. The feet should move lightly and easily across the ground, moving on the balls of the feet as much as possible.

There are two forms of *tai no shintai*, or body movement; *ayumi ashi*, corresponding to ordinary walking and *tsugi ashi*, or glide walking.

## AYUMI ASHI

*Ayumi ashi* is a form of walking, in that the feet pass each other, each foot alternating in the lead. It differs from our normal walking in the street, by requiring the feet to glide on the balls of the feet, maintaining contact with the ground at all times. It is important also to point the feet to the outside to increase stability and to take measured steps that maintain the body's centre of gravity. Thus the back is held straight and head upright in good posture. *Ayumi ashi*, with variations in the positioning of the feet, is a familiar method of walking in many Japanese martial sword and weapon arts and is used logically, to cover longer distances across the *dojo*.

## TSUGI ASHI

*Tsugi ashi* is the most common movement of entry into the application of a technique. It is performed as a glide, or perhaps more descriptively a slide across the mats, both feet moving almost simultaneously. In this action the right foot is moved forward, with the left foot sliding quickly forward behind it so that both feet are planted at the same time, to halt in *migi kamae*. Naturally, when the left foot leads, the body will move into *hidari kamae*. Once again all the elements of good posture must pertain, with the torso remaining upright and centred in *sankakutai*, or triangular form, framed by the positioning of the feet. All students will place particular emphasis on learning to move quickly and instinctively in these patterns and each school has its own drills and exercises to encourage acquisition of this skill.

Learning to walk in the *dojo* might seem to be a simple skill, easily acquired. This is far from the truth, as every beginner to aikido soon discovers. For it means unlearning, for the purposes of aikido, all our unconscious, habitual patterns of movement to adopt two very specific, and in relation to everyday life, unnatural ways of walking. Early awkwardness is expected and soon resolved through application to training, giving grace and form to the movement of the *aikidoka* across the mat. This training will have its spin off in improvements to our posture outside the *dojo*. In aikido as in life, learning to walk is the opening to experience.

## SHIKKO (WALKING ON THE KNEES)

As we have seen, part of the practice of aikido involves the performance of techniques from the seated position of *seiza*,

which are known as *suwari waza*. To receive an attack from this position and counter it with an aikido technique, requires you to walk on your knees, in a swift, graceful manner. This was a form of walking necessary to formal behaviour, in a society that lived its domestic life on mats. Not that the necessity for such an ability has disappeared in modern Japanese life, for despite the popularity of modern furniture, many Japanese homes, restaurants, temples and public buildings retain the traditional *tatami*, straw mat floors.

Aikido acknowledges that the likelihood of your having to defend yourself from this posture is, certainly in the West, very remote. However, the practice is continued for the practical purpose of developing stability and a strong sense of being grounded in your *tanden*, the centre point of your body. *Shikko* also helps to develop power in the hips, vital to executing any technique, kneeling or standing.

## UKEMI (FALLING)

There is no doubt that the most uncomfortable and off-putting element of aikido training for the beginner is learning how to fall. Fear of falling is a natural and sane human instinct which we have learnt through the course of our lives. It is the purpose of *ukemi*, or breakfall training, to unlearn this accumulated experience and return us to the easy and relaxed relationship we once had with the ground when we were young.

The simple purpose of *ukemi* is to train the body to meet the ground with the whole body and spirit, rather than trying to avoid the fall and consequently taking all the shock on one awkward point, such as a wrist or elbow. The ability to fall skilfully and recover one's feet, all in one flowing, seamless motion gives the student confidence to explore all the vital aspects of a throw or technique. Thus it is important not only to learn how to do a technique, but to learn also how it feels. This will be a factor when training with senior and more experienced *aikidoka*. For often, understanding of how a technique works comes only when you have found yourself on the end of a correctly executed throw, and discovered at which precise angle and moment your body was unable to recover its posture. If you are in fear of the floor below you, then you will not be centred and able to learn or act in the drama of the aikido encounter with a free and open mind.

Falling is a central element of aikido practice. Any lesson will require falling and returning to the feet more times than, as a beginner, you may wish. Your confidence and ability in *ukemi* is not only important to your own progress but it is of equal importance to your partner. The shared experience in the *dojo*, means that *nage's* ability to execute a technique at the highest level is dependent on *uke's* ability to receive it. Your skill will contribute to your partner's progress as theirs will to yours. Through this mutual commitment we learn to fall 'seven times and get up eight'.

The moral principle we take with us into our lives from our practice of *ukemi*, is that we must learn to take setbacks or failure with our whole personality and know we have the resilience and will to come to our feet once again.

Aikido breakfalls take these basic forms; *zenpo kaiten* (forward rolling fall), *koho ukemi* (backward rolling fall), and *yoko ukemi*, or falls to the side and variations linked to techniques such as *kote gaeshi* (wrist twist), where your wrist will be held by your partner until you reach the ground. Space precludes giving a detailed description of each breakfall and its component elements and is best left to instruction in the *dojo*, where the teacher, or *sensei*, will introduce the varieties of breakfall in un-threatening, easy steps. However, it is important to stress the principle of the circle that underlies the philosophy and practice of aikido.

Like water, aikido seeks the easiest passage through space.

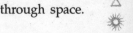

The easiest way to the floor and up again is to minimise contact with it. In a forward rolling breakfall this is accomplished by taking a forward step with the right foot, bending the knee and trunk low while stretching the left leg behind. Curving the right arm forward to place the *tegatana*, or edge of your hand, to make contact with the mat, you form an extended curve from the edge of your hand, running along your arm and over your head. To avoid injury, your head is turned to the left and tucked into the body between your left arm and the mat, looking back towards your left ankle. In one fluid motion you roll forward along the arc formed by the curve of your right arm, along your shoulder, and across your back like the effortless turn of a wheel.

Once learnt, *ukemi* forms an important psychological prop to your training, freeing you to concentrate and develop your skills without fear of injury. Hopefully, this skill will become instinctive and increase your confidence in other areas of life both physically, when confronting the risk of falling, and spiritually, when confronting failure and potential defeat.

## HARMONY IN ACTION:
## THE PRACTICE OF TECHNIQUE

The principle part of any aikido lesson must of course be the practice of aikido *waza* or techniques themselves. The principles of movement on which aikido is based and a full description of their physical character will be given later in this book. At this point our focus is upon the context in which the learning of aikido takes place.

The teaching of aikido bases its teaching of technique on partner practice where an attacker's assault is countered and subdued by a defender employing aikido *waza*. Unlike the development of punching and kicking skills, which can be performed against the air or a punch bag, the elements of aikido technique require physical contact. The aim of aikido *waza* is to neutralize an opponent by throwing him to the ground, or forcing the opponent to the ground and restraining him by the use of joint-locks which put compelling pressure on the wrist, elbow or shoulder. Although the practice of the individual components of a *waza* can be mimed solo for reinforcement, it is impossible to learn aikido technique without physically manipulating a partner.

The prearranged sets of actions and sequences of movement that compose aikido *waza* have to be learned in a situation of trust. Each partner takes it in turn to perform as *nage*, the one who executes the technique, and *uke*, the one who receives the technique. In the aikido *dojo* the practice of *waza* is a shared relationship of equals, where selfishness or gratuitous aggression must be purged to avoid injury for both one's partner and ones self. Injury must be seen as spiritual as much as it is physical.

Yet, this relationship must have purpose and some degree of realism within the context of a martial moment or event, for real learning to take place. For although *budo*, or the martial Way, has replaced the *samurai*'s 'sport of death' with the 'sport of life', the practice of technique must retain some element of danger. Attacks must be pressed home to equip the *aikidoka* with a sense of timing and speed of response; techniques must be applied correctly and decisively. To gain any appreciation of classical *budo*'s emphasis on *seishi o choetsu*, or 'transcending' thought about life or death', then we must imagine this as combat. Both *nage* and *uke* must understand that the techniques we practise can harm, and potentially kill. Our responsibility during this combat is to maintain a strict discipline and purpose ensuring that we defend ourselves and the integrity of our own person and character without damaging the integrity of our partner. Therefore, within the *dojo* there are no winners or losers. The practice of *waza* is a shared experience where students 'learn the reality of inter-dependence'. The partner practise method is as a consequence, an important tool for building social tolerance and harmony between individuals, serving both as a means to understand and model a technique physically, while at the same time modelling the ethics of aikido and inflicting no harm or humiliation on one's opponent.

With the exception of *Tomiki Aikido*, where it forms an important part of its teaching methodology, aikido *waza* are not grouped in linked sequences of techniques or *kata*. Each *waza* is demonstrated and learned individually, although each has its variations according to the manner and circumstances of attack. The techniques, or *waza*, are the vocabulary of aikido from which we learn to construct a dialogue of movement with our partner. Just as with spoken language we begin to construct sentences and conduct conversations, so with the learning of *waza* the grammar of aikido is constructed and we are eventually able to speak for ourselves.

Our guide through this process is, of course, our teacher or *sensei*. He or she will demonstrate the technique and break down its components for us to mirror as accurately as we can, and move around the *dojo* to analyse our faults, correct our posture, encourage and praise. The teacher will not only be concerned to see us perform the technique effectively, but will be drawing out our appreciation of the *waza* form as an aesthetic experience. Good technique is beautiful technique, demonstrating economy and grace of movement, rhythm and flow in a fleeting choreographed moment. Through the development of our understanding of this combination of the technical, ethical and aesthetic components which make up a technique, we gain insight into the mind of aikido. We begin to develop our own aikido mind itself and learn to act spontaneously and appropriately in moments of stress, and to conduct our affairs with dignity and good grace.

At the closing of practice all aikido clubs will call for a period of warming down to readjust the body temperature and keep the limbs flexible. These warming down exercises will be idiosyncratic and do not conform to a particular pattern as they form no part of the curriculum *per se*. However, some teachers may use elements of *aiki taiso* (exercises) involving the twisting of joints or other basic exercises in their programme. Some classes will concentrate on stretching exercises, to take advantage of a truly warmed body, as flexibility is the key fitness element for the *aikidoka*. Whatever your current level of fitness or flexibility, no one will expect you to attempt exercises beyond your range. A well run class under an experienced *sensei* (teacher), will encourage your efforts and build pace and stamina at the incremental rate with which you can cope. Aikido does not require the development of biceps or calloused hands, only a good level of natural fitness.

## THE LINE, AND THE IMPORTANCE OF PLACE

The aikido session will end as it began with the teacher calling students to form a line, each *aikidoka* taking their place in line according to rank or grade. Aikido, in common with all modern *budo*, has adopted the *kyu/dan* system of ranking, which recognises the progress of an *aikidoka* through training. Periodic tests or gradings are held to assess the skills and maturity in the art, against standards that are expected at different levels of experience. Time and frequency of practice, allied to a mature and patient mind are the elements most likely to assure progress. Good teachers guide the student through this process, so that they are never required to test for a grade before they are ready.

Ranks in aikido are demonstrated by the wearing of belts, which change in colour with progress through the ranks. Beginners usually start with a red or white belt and move up through a number of *kyu* grades, ranging from five to eight or more. Moving from 1st *kyu* to *shodan* (first *dan*) wins the coveted black belt and further progression through *dan* (black belt) rankings.

Gradings are not an essential element of the practice of aikido. Morihei Ueshiba, *O Sensei*, came rather reluctantly to their use in his system, but eventually conformed to the mood of the times. Their advantage lies only in how much they may act as an incentive for students to focus on raising the level of their practice, to meet a particular goal, or target. They also have a spin-off in that their visibility, as different coloured belts for different grades, allows students to match the intensity and technical complexity of their practice to the level each can cope with. This is useful when training in unfamiliar *dojo*, where your level of skill may be unknown. As a rule of thumb, it is always better to train with *aikidoka* senior to you. They will not only teach you as much as they can, but will, through experience, be calmer and more considerate in the application of technique.

In addition to the black belt, *dan* grades and some dojo women of lower grades may wear a *hakama*. *Hakama* are classical Japanese divided culottes trousers, black or dark blue in colour, worn in respect of tradition and for the flowing, swirling grace they give to the performance of aikido at its higher levels. Much pride and care is taken with this training garment and at the conclusion of training it will be folded away with great precision and tied with a traditional knot.

Taking your place in the line is not a practice to resent. It is not meant to put you in your place, or humiliate the beginners at the lower end of the line. It is for you to mark your place and to measure your progress along the path. Above you are your *sempai*, or seniors, whose responsibility it is to help and guide you and provide the extra support and encouragement that you may require. Very quickly, others will follow you and you

will find yourself with *kohai*, or juniors, that you in your turn must look out for, as your seniors looked after you and your training. The good *dojo* survives on the care and concern exercised by its students and its success in creating a community of learning, with a mutual passion for aikido.

## MOKUSO AND THE CONCLUDING RITUAL

When the line in order of grade is established, a senior student will call to the class to kneel in *seiza* and commence *mokuso*. The concluding ritual is the mirror of the opening ceremony. At this moment *mokuso* serves to return you from the physical and mental challenges you have faced, through deep abdominal breathing to a state of meditative calm. In these moments through emptying your mind you seek to internalize what you have learnt and clear space for new events.

*Zarei*, followed by ritual clapping for the attention of the *kami* of aikido and the bow to O *Sensei's* picture on the *kamiza* wall, gives thanks to the teacher, the tradition in which you practise, your fellow students and most importantly, Morihei Ueshiba who has given us the gift of aikido.

All that will now be required is to follow your teacher and fellow students from the *tatami*, bowing out of the *dojo* with *ritsu-rei*, until the cycle of training returns you once more to the *dojo* door.

# HOW THE TECHNIQUES WORK: ENTERING AND TURNING

A s we have seen, aikido's technical roots can be found in the systems of close quarter combat known generically as *jujutsu*. Of these systems, the *Daito Ryu Aiki jujutsu* school of Sokaku Takeda with whom Morihei Ueshiba studied for many years was the prime source and inspiration for his own aikido. This inheritance, together with some characteristic principles of sword practice assimilated from the *Kashima Shinto Ryu* (a 500 year old school of weapon arts), forms the technical root of aikido. Ueshiba's genius was not only to give this tradition a new ethical and moral dimension, emphasising the redeeming qualities of serious *budo* study, but, by transforming the character and execution of the techniques, he made a unity of thought and deed.

Within the components of the Chinese character *Bu*, can be read, *Ko o yameru* or the cessation of arms. *Budo* therefore, can be seen as a means for preserving *wa*, or harmony in the defence of the public good. Aikido, goes beyond the Classical *budo* concept, 'to take one life to save many', to a belief that one can defend social harmony and yet still preserve the life and human integrity of one's opponent. Aikido seeks then to exploit the physical means by which an opponent can be subdued, with minimal disturbance and effort, in the interests of preserving *wa*, or harmony and the cessation of discord.

For this philosophical conviction to become a reality in action, a long developmental process was undergone, reflecting the stages of spiritual growth experienced by the founder, Morihei Ueshiba, during his life-time. Early pre-World War II students of *O Sensei*, were subject to a tough regime, where a robust *aiki jujutsu* was taught in a manner that had deviated little from that taught by Sokaku Takeda. Later post-WWII students, were to see a new aikido that had been forged through the bitter war years, during Ueshiba *Sensei's* self imposed isolation on his farm at Iwama. This was undoubtedly a softer aikido, more fluid and graceful and yet devastatingly effective against single and multiple assailants alike.

## MARUI: CIRCULAR MOTION

This 'new' aikido was developed by exploitation of the principle of *marui*, or circular motion, to take advantage of the opponent's physical strength to defeat them. There are few straight lines in aikido, the movement of feet, arms and torso describe circles and arcs in all dimensions, conforming to the shape of a sphere or spiral. The *aikidoka* thus becomes the centre of a centripetal or centrifugal force, alternately drawing opponents into a whirlpool that brings them spiralling to the ground, or throws them off like objects colliding with a spinning globe.

By definition, movements through space that follow these principles involve continuous flowing motion, uninterrupted by the awkward, angular changes that are required by moving in straight lines. Thus, in executing a technique, the *aikidoka* may seek to pivot out of his opponent's oncoming path, adding his own strength and power to that of the assailant, to control or throw them, rather than directly to confront or clash in a futile test of strength.

# JU: FLEXIBILITY

To this application of the dynamics of circular motion is welded aikido's interpretation of the principle of flexibility, or *ju*. In the close grappling arts such as judo, this principle is demonstrated when, if you are pushed by an opponent, you pull to unbalance him. This adds your pulling strength to their pushing strength, instead of wasting energy and power by trying to oppose his force with your own. If on the other hand, your opponent is trying to pull you, then the opposite principle takes effect and you must push to unbalance him. Following the principle of circular motion, aikido's axiom becomes, when pushed, 'turn' and when pulled, 'enter' or follow. It is in this way that the *aiki-doka* seeks to move with the direction of the attack, adding his own power and momentum to the opponent's force, to break their posture, unbalance and control them.

## AIKIDO TECHNIQUE:
## THE SHAPE AND FORM OF AIKIDO

Aikido technique is divided into categories that correspond to the relative body positioning of the attacker, *uke*, and the defender, *nage*, and the manner of defence by throwing, controlling or striking an opponent. These body positions are defined as:

- *Suwari waza*, where both *nage* and *uke* are seated in *seiza*.
- *Hanmi hantachi waza*, where *nage is* seated and *uke* is standing
- and *tachi waza*, where both *nage* and *uke* are standing.

The categories of technique are divided into:

- *Atemi waza,* striking or impact applied against physiological weaknesses.
- *Katame waza,* where *uke* is controlled by *nage* by means of anatomical pressure on the wrist, elbow and shoulder joints.
- *Nage waza,* where *uke* is thrown to the ground by *nage.*

While these remain the major technical divisions, further categories exist for techniques applied to more than one opponent and to opponents armed with the *tanto,* or knife, the *ken* or sword and the *jo,* or staff. While it is possible to define the categories of technique and general principles that they follow, it would be impossible to describe each and every one. In a sense they are limitless, as each encounter creates its own dynamic with which the *aikidoka* attempts to harmonise; adapting and extemporising the application of *waza,* to suit the individual circumstances of the moment. At its highest level, *aikido* could be said to be beyond technique and have become an intuitive and creative interpretation of circular energy and the exploitation of physiological and anatomical weaknesses. It is the practical expression of *ki.*

This book is not intended to be an instructional manual and will not attempt to do more than give a few examples of techniques within the categories described, in order to give the reader a broader understanding of how they work. Those who may be interested in pursuing the study of aikido after reading this book, will be best served by seeking out a *dojo* and a teacher and trying it for themselves. There is never any substitute for experience.

## THE STRATEGY OF APPLICATION

All basic technique may be broken down into essential elements, relating to phases in their application. These are:

- *Maai,* or the control of space to deny or gain advantage.
- *Taisabaki,* or body positioning, to avoid attack and manoeuvre to make an effective counter response.
- *Tsukuri,* or structuring, whereby the skilful use of eye-contact *(metsuke)* posture, hand movements and unbalancing *(kuzushi),* are combined to enable:
- *Kake,* the application of the throw *(nage),* or joint-lock *(katame waza)* where *uke* is thrown to the ground and subdued.
- *Zanshin,* or 'lingering spirit', where *nage* focuses his concentration and remaining posture over his fallen opponent, subduing uke's will to resist further.

These elements are combined according to the principles of aikido, using *tenkan,* or turning motion, *irimi,* or entering, or *kaiten,* to enter and turn in combination. By utilizing these movements the *aikidoka* is able to blend, *awase,* with the opponent's direction of movement and manner of attack. All through the action, a calm centre is maintained through the use of *kokyu,* or breath power.

## TENKAN

*Tenkan* is the movement by which *nage,* the defender, pivots away from the incoming path of *uke*'s attack, by pivoting on one foot and drawing the other in a circular arc around him to face in the opposite direction. *Uke*'s attack can be simply avoided by this move, or controlled and redirected around *nage.* It is important for *nage* to have a firm centre and good posture when performing this manoeuvre, to prevent the whirlpool of *uke*'s energy unbalancing him.

## IRIMI

*Irimi* is an entering movement designed to bring *nage,* the defender, in close to *uke*'s, the attacker's, body without meeting in a head-on clash. The principle is simple and effective, only requiring *nage* to move off line and forward at a sharp angle into the safe side of *uke*'s body. By using this movement, *nage* is able to move out of the direct line of attack and cut forward into *uke*'s centre or rear to take the advantage.

## KAITEN: OPEN AND TURN, (OR IRIMI TENKAN: ENTER AND TURN)

*Kaiten* is the demonstration of the principle of *marui*, or circular motion in action. It is essentially the exploitation of the geometry of movement, based on the patterns woven by enveloping circles and arcs described by the inter-connecting paths of *nage* and *uke*. As *uke* moves forward and *nage* opens or enters to the side of the direct line of attack and then turns around it in a circular arc, *uke* is drawn around the central pivot which *nage* has become, and his aggressive energy is dissipated. Alternatively, *nage* may choose to move around the outer perimeter of *uke*'s circle before entering *uke*'s centre to overwhelm him.

As we have noted before these circles do not all lie on the horizontal. They can also be described through the air, as a spiral that spins *uke* to the ground or a circle in the vertical plane that wheels *uke* over *nage*'s body to the floor. The substance of the principle is the redirection of *uke*'s power, without halting the flow of energy. *Uke*'s power is lost in his commitment to the action and he finds himself rushing forward against no opposition, until, guided by *nage*'s energy matching his own, he is neutralized with a technique.

## AWASE

*Awase* is one of the most difficult concepts to describe as it cannot be defined in any one physical action. Rather it is the quest of aikido to make *awase* present in all actions. The term *awase*, comes from the verb *awaseru*, to blend or harmonize and

is a physical demonstration of the spiritual harmony for which aikido strives. *Awase*, is a mental skill or sensitivity, which allows the *aikidoka* to match movement to movement, timing to timing, the actions of his opponent rather than directly confronting them. When *awase* is successfully utilized in a technique, then it will seem to the aggressor that he has been thrown by some unseen force or otherwise inexplicably fallen to the ground on his own account.

## KOKYU (BREATH)

*Kokyu* is, as we have described above, the power to summon and regulate the breath to keep it even and smoothly flowing throughout any encounter, however stressful. Ideally, the body and mind will learn to breath in when beginning the technique and out when executing the technique, to give it power and energy.

## ATTACKS IN AIKIDO

Attacks in aikido cover the likely forms and directions of an assault. These are:

- *Shomen uchi* a strike with the knife hand, *tegatana*, to the centre of the head.
- *Yokomen uchi*, *migi* (right) or *hidari* (left) a strike with the knife hand, *tegatana*, to the side of the head.
- *Tsuki* a punch or thrust to the stomach, chest or face.
- *Katate dori* where one hand is seized and held by *uke*.
- *Ryote dori* where both hands are seized and held by *uke*.
- *Kata dori* where *nage's* shoulder is seized and held by *uke*.
- *Morote dori* where *nage's* arm is seized and held by *uke* with two hands.
- *Ushiro dori*, where nage is seized and held from behind by *uke*.

At first these attacks may seem stylised and lacking in pace and conviction. However, the pace and power of an attack is established by *nage*'s ability to deal effectively, smoothly, and above all safely, with it. As the student progresses, so will his ability to deal with swifter and fiercer attacks, whatever the size and temper of the opponent. *Nage* is never overwhelmed by having to think of a counter and then move. Actions become instinctive and ingrained, as each move is continuously rehearsed until speed and timing are perfected.

These formal attacks may be supplemented in some *dojo*, with *karate* kicks, such as *mae geri* (front kick) and *mawashi geri* (side kick), to promote an aikido that is still a realistic means of self-defence.

## DEFENCE IN AIKIDO

In defence against attack, the *aikidoka* will choose to employ a technique from; *atemi waza* (striking vital points), *katame waza* (joint-locks and controls), or *nage waza* (throws). The manner, direction and speed of the attack and whether you are facing a weapon, such as a knife, or more than one opponent, will all have a bearing on the choices made. If you are facing assault from more than one opponent, then a technique which involves having to pin or control one opponent, will not leave you free to defend yourself against another. In circumstances such as these, dispatching your attackers quickly with strikes and throws would be the most effective. However, if you are required to defend yourself against a lone assailant, who may be drunk or otherwise offensive, then it would be better to restrain and control him with a joint-lock until calm is restored.

Often, these categories do not divide themselves simply, and the *aikidoka*, will deploy a combination of techniques, following an escalating pattern of response. Let us take a particular example; the collar is seized as the prelude to delivering a punch to the face. The *aikidoka's* initial reaction would be to manoeuvre to avoid the blow, and position himself ready for an effective counter. Simultaneously the *taisabaki* move is accompanied by a strike, to the face or another weak point on the opponent's body. The strike is intended to inflict sharp pain, not in the expectation that this will end the encounter, but more to serve as a distraction. This will provide the time for the *aikidoka* to apply a joint lock on the opponent's wrist.

Aikido locks are devastatingly effective. Working with the natural flexibility of the joint, rather than opposing it, the joint's range of manoeuvre is stressed until its limits are reached, causing acute pain. This results in a loss of stability and concentration by the attacker and a further opening for the *aikidoka* to throw or bring the opponent to the ground by the controlling use of pain applied through the joint-lock itself. At each stage, the opportunity to halt the escalation is present, if the opponent is ready to concede.

Skilful technique is the essential responsibility of the peaceful urban warrior. It will enable you to have both the confidence in your ability to preserve yourself, and the option to make ethical choices about the degree of damage applied by you in your defence. In a litigious age, over reactive defence can have unexpected and unwelcome consequences within the law. Aikido, with its strong ethical character and strategy of appropriate escalation, can confidently address this issue.

# KIHON WAZA: FUNDAMENTAL TECHNIQUE

## ATEMI WAZA

The use of *atemi waza*, or the striking of vital points, within aikido cannot be equated with the familiar media influenced perception of martial arts such as karate and the Korean *taekwondo*, which are primarily punching and kicking arts. The function of *atemi waza* within aikido is not to orchestrate a combination of blows and thereby inflict damage and knock out an opponent, but to strike against physiological weak points, or take advantage of an opponent's loss of balance to *throw* him down.

Systematic teaching of *atemi* strikes, intended to inflict severe injury, has largely disappeared from aikido *dojo* around the world. The emphasis has shifted from narrow concerns of self-defence to broader aesthetic and cultural considerations. However, the use of distracting strikes to the head, to the side of the head or to the bridge of the nose in the form of a *metsub-ushi*, or smashing eye-blow delivered by the back of the fist, regularly precede the application of a joint-lock. This has particular relevance when seized by an opponent from front or behind, where a strike to your opponent's face or an elbow to his ribs can cause that moment of confusion and loss of balance that you can exploit.

*Atemi*, which exploits an opponent's momentary loss of balance to apply force in one direction, against one point of his body, to throw him down, is that most commonly found in the aikido repertoire. This form of *atemi*, requires no particular strength or special exercises to harden the knuckles or edges of the hands. Aikido *atemi* relies on timing and the proper use of movement and body alignment, to thrust or strike an opponent just as he is in movement and his own balance is insecure. This often follows a *taisabaki* or avoidance manoeuvre made by the *aikidoka*. It leaves the opponent momentarily thwarted and on the 'wrong-foot', as when a deflecting block may have caused him to over-reach or stumble.

The *irimi*, or entering movement, is much employed in this context. The *aikidoka* will come off-line to avoid the opponent's on-coming path and move forward into him. He will transfer his weight to front knee and catch him with a thrust to chin or shoulder just as the opponent's foot lifts or descends and his balance is unsettled. Within aikido, *atemi* is understood to mean more than delivering a blow with fist or hand. It includes any contact made with the opponent using timing and focused energy and is delivered with any part of the body that applies force in one direction to throw him to the ground.

This use of the principle of *atemi* can be seen in the throwing technique described below where *nage*, the thrower, both thrusts and cuts with his hands, moving in the direction of *uke's* loss of posture.

### TENCHI NAGE: HEAVEN AND EARTH THROW

*Basic Principles*

This technique is named for one hand is 'leading up to the heavens' while the other attempts to 'pierce the earth'. When *uke* grasps *nage's* hands attempting to force them apart, *nage* reinforces this movement, screwing his right hand forward and lifting it in a circular direction above his head. This action lifts *uke's* left hand from the inside. At the same moment *nage* moves his body to the left and cuts down with his left hand (*tegatana*), to *uke's* right rear, thus disturbing *uke's* balance.

With *uke's* shoulder as the pivot point, *nage* continues to push upward with his right hand and cut downward with his left hand, moving forward with his right leg (or knee in *suwari waza* application) to *uke's* right rear. *Uke* is lifted upward and round to his right rear in a circular motion, until he falls (from the standing position), or is pressed to the mat (from the kneeling position).

# RYOTE DORI TENCHI NAGE:
## GRASPED HANDS HEAVEN AND EARTH THROW
## COMMENTARY: TACHI WAZA (STANDING TECHNIQUE)

*Nage* and *uke* stand in neutral posture facing each other. Uke advances to grasp *nage's* hands. Uke grasps *nage's* hands. *Nage* immediately responds, extending his right hand palm up towards *uke's* left shoulder, cutting his left hand down to *uke's* right rear.

Tenchi Nage

*Nage* continues the drive forwards, advancing his right foot and screwing his right hand round and upward against *uke's* left shoulder. *Uke's* left hand is lifted and his posture is broken to the right rear. *Nage* lifts *uke* over his right hip, sweeping round and down with his right hand. *Uke's* balance is completely broken and he is lifted off his feet. *Uke* performs a breakfall, or *ukemi* and *nage* maintains *zanshin*.

## KATAME WAZA: TWISTING AND LOCKING THE JOINTS OF THE BODY

The joints of the human body as we all know are natural points of weakness, receiving much stress and strain from our normal everyday activities. Accidents can cause even more severe stress, particularly when the joint has been made to do something it was never intended to do. Many traditional *jujutsu* and wrestling holds in Greco-Roman or Eastern traditions apply pressure to a joint in opposition to its natural direction of movement. The intention is to break or dislocate an arm or leg at this weak point.

Aikido *katame waza*, or joint locking techniques, generally work in the opposite direction by twisting the joint the way it naturally wants to go, but taking it that bit further than it can cope with. The consequences are as severe, often more so, than by opposing the joint. The advantages of exploiting the anatomy of the body in this way lie in the ease with which the joint can be turned without having to wrench it into an unnatural position. Although an aikido lock or control causes acute pain when applied, it does less damage to the joint. Once the aikido lock is released the pain subsides, while stress *against* a joint can cause continuing pain and potential long term damage.

We can see that working with this natural range of movement prescribes the character of *katame* technique, as there is an obvious and limited number of directions in which the wrist and elbow can be twisted. All these techniques begin from a grasp or counter-grasp of an opponent's wrist or forearm, even if the final lock is applied to the elbow or shoulder. The wrist may then be twisted, or the arm turned over, by applying pressure and circular movement to the wrist, to the elbow, or to both, in order to take down or throw an opponent.

An important characteristic of aikido's *katame waza* is that when *uke* is brought to the ground, he is face down to the floor and held there by the controlled application of pain to an anatomical weak point. Providing that *uke* does not struggle, then minimal pain or hurt will be experienced. If *uke* does attempt to struggle free, then *nage* will instantly apply pressure on the joint or weak point to subdue him. This gives *nage* the opportunity to exercise compassion in the application of a joint-locking hold down, as he need only inflict minimal pain and discomfort to control *uke*. Any escalation of severity is, in a sense, the responsibility of *uke* and can be introduced incrementally by *nage* to remind his opponent of the pain and discomfort his resistance risks.

This is in contradistinction to judo and other *jujutsu* styles, where *uke* is most often held down on his back by the weight and pressure of *nage*'s body on top of him, restricting his movement and ease of breathing. To supplement these physical hold downs there is a sophisticated range of choking and strangling techniques designed to cut off the supply of blood to the brain and ultimately bring unconsciousness. This requires considerable exertion on both *nage* and *uke*'s part and is a continuation of the close grappling character of judo on the floor.

Aikido has discarded this element of classical *jujutsu* or judo technique from its curriculum, eschewing any grappling or contention on the floor. Aikido relies instead on techniques that can be applied from a standing or kneeling position to keep *uke* pinned face down to the floor.

# WHEN IS THERE AN OPPORTUNITY TO USE KATAME WAZA?

To apply *katame waza* techniques you must first be able to get hold of an opponent's forearm or wrist before trying to turn them backwards or twist them forwards. No opponent is likely to stand still while you calmly seize hold of them, so you must be ready to take advantage of one of three important opportunities.

- You have deflected *uke's* attack with your *tegatana*, or hand-blade and broken their balance.
- *Uke* has got hold of you and seized your arm, wrist, collar, sleeve, shoulder or any other part of your person.
- *Uke* has parried a blow (a *metsubushi*, or blinding blow) you have struck to his head or face with his forearm or hand-blade. Or your opponent has been startled by your blow and you have an opportunity to seize his wrist or forearm.

In each case your opponent has been placed in a state of inaction for a brief moment. It is this opportunity that the *aikidoka* must exploit to grasp the opponent's forearm and initiate a *katame waza* technique.

## HOW KATAME WAZA WORKS

*Katame waza*, to summarize, are techniques used to throw or hold down an opponent by attacking weak points in the joints of the body. Kenji Tomiki, one of *O Sensei's* most prominent students, offers a useful model for analysing *katame waza*, according to the physiological processes which they exploit. Tomiki's model sees all *katame waza* techniques as being broadly based on two key physiological observations:

- When the body's balance is gradually broken forward (with the weight of the body shifting to the toes and the body inclining forward), the elbow joints rise and the forearms turn inward.

- When the body's balance is gradually broken backward (with the weight of the body shifting to the heels and the body inclining backward), the elbow joints lower and the forearms turn outward.

Thus, if you wish to break an opponent's balance there are two basic principles. You can:

- Break an opponent's balance forward by twisting his arm inward;
- Break an opponent's balance backward by twisting his arm outward.

By grasping and twisting the opponent's wrist or arm, according to these two principles, you are able to break an opponent's posture with the minimum of physical effort. When the posture is broken it is possible to throw and hold him down with a technique, again with little physical strength required.

*Katame waza* can be sub-divided into two major categories:

- *Hiji-waza*, or techniques that attack the elbow joints, and are applied against a stretched arm, or when the arm is entangled and the arm bent.
- *Tekubi-waza*, or techniques that attack vulnerable points in the wrist joints, and can be further sub-divided into two categories; variations of *kote hineri* (wrist twist, inward), where, as a result of this twisting, *uke*'s balance is broken to the front, and *kote gaeshi* (wrist turn, outward), where, as a result of turning the wrist, *uke*'s balance is broken to the rear.

# HOW YOU APPLY KATAME WAZA

To illustrate these principles in practice two basic techniques have been chosen. They demonstrate, in the first case an attack against the opponent's elbow, twisting it inward to break his posture to the front; and in the second example, turning the wrist outward to break the posture to the rear.

## HIJI WAZA:
### IKKYO (BREAKING BALANCE FORWARD AND PINNING THE STRETCHED ARM)

*Basic Principles*

*Ikkyo*, or first teaching, is a control applied against the elbow. The elbow is grasped and turned over (to the inside) in a descending arc to break *uke*'s balance and bring him face down to the floor. When taken to the ground, *uke* is pinned and prevented from moving by pressure applied directly to the elbow joint by *nage*'s hand, which is the *ikkyo* pin itself. The technique can be used both to control and pin *uke* to the floor, or propel him down to the ground as a throw.

To perform this technique, one must be in firm control of one's centre to be able to apply power directly down onto *uke*'s elbow. This can be illustrated by the application *suwari waza shomen uchi ikkyo osae*, where *nage* is attacked with a front strike to the head from a kneeling position. He defeats this action, by subduing *uke* with an *ikkyo* pin to the elbow.

### SUWARI WAZA SHOMEN UCHI IKKYO OSAE:
### COMMENTARY

*Uke* and *nage* sit in *seiza*, facing each other. *Uke* rises onto his or her toes to make a front strike, *shomen uchi*, to *nage*'s head with his right hand. *Nage* responds simultaneously with *uke*'s action, rising onto his own toes and raising his right *tegatana* hand-blade to block *uke*'s descending strike before it has any momentum.

Suwari waza shomen uchi ikkyo osae

At the same time *nage* grasps *uke's* elbow with his left hand. *Nage* grips *uke's* right wrist and elbow and turns them over, rotating them in an arc towards *uke's* head. *Uke's* elbow is rotated over his head and shoulder to his left rear, turning him around and breaking his balance.

*Nage* maintains a firm grip on *uke's* wrist, applying downward pressure on *uke's* elbow with his left hand and driving his knee at a 45° angle across *uke's* body. As *uke* is forced to the floor *nage* pushes his knee firmly into *uke's* armpit and stretches *uke's* arm out (knuckles down). *Nage* completes the pin by pressing down on *uke's* elbow joint. The back is straightened and the lower abdomen pushed down toward the mat with the whole weight of the body transferred through *nage's* arm to *uke's* elbow, separating and stretching the joint.

## TEKUBI WAZA:

### KOTE GAESHI (BREAKING BALANCE TO THE REAR)

*Basic Principles*

*Kote gaeshi* is one of aikido's most dramatic forms, where the application of the principles of timing and circular movement come together with a simple turn of an opponent's wrist to throw him to the ground. The drama is effected by *uke's* spectacular use of *ukemi* (breakfalls) to escape the consequences of this simple lock, propelling him in a high circular arc over his own wrist to land on his back.

### TSUKI KOTEGAESHI: COMMENTARY

*Uke* and *nage*, face each other in left *ai-hanmi* (mutual oblique position). *Uke* drives forward with *tsuki*, a straight thrusting punch with the right fist. *Nage* moves forward and to the outside of *uke's* attack, turning (*tenkan*) and deflecting *uke's* blow with his left *tegatana*, (hand-blade) and breaks *uke's* balance forward. Seizing this opportunity *nage* grasps *uke's* right wrist

Tsuki Kotegaeshi

PRINCIPLES OF AIKIDO

with the left hand. The little and second finger are placed on the inside of the wrist, and the thumb firmly placed in the middle of the back of *uke*'s hand. This move is reinforced by applying pressure to the back of *uke*'s hand with *nage*'s right hand placed over his thumb. *Nage* moves forward onto the right foot and turns, simultaneously turning *uke*'s wrist to the outside and applying downward pressure, breaking *uke*'s posture backwards. To escape the consequences of the lock, *uke* performs *ukemi* and falls safely.

## THE PRINCIPLES OF SWORDSMANSHIP

Aikido is most often seen as an unarmed martial way, sharing with modern judo the common ancestry of classical *jujutsu* principles of flexibility and the redirection of opposing force. But here the comparison ends. What distinguishes aikido from other unarmed martial arts is the application of technique according to the 'principles of swordsmanship'. Thus, the movement of hands, the central alignment of torso and hips, the positioning of the feet and *maai*, the spatial relationship between yourself and your opponent all conform to the principles of classical sword-play. The *tegatana*, or sword-hand, is wielded in the manner of a sword, cutting down from above the head or thrusting upward, utilizing the power of *chushin*, or central alignment, to deliver a decisive *atemi* technique.

These principles can be observed in the use of the *tegatana*, substituting for the sword, to both deflect and parry. This is often followed by a sweeping cut across *uke*'s body which destroys his stability and forms the basis for throwing him down. However, it is the strategic application of these principles that is of primary importance. It is in the judgement of distance, the quick movement off-line and darting entry into an opponents defensive space that the elements of swordsmanship can be judged.

Ueshiba *O Sensei* saw swordsmanship as a vital element of *budo* training and spent many long hours practising with his *bokken*, the wooden training sword familiar to practitioners of Japanese *kenjutsu* and its modern *shin budo* form kendo.

He attached great importance to training with the sword, both for himself and for his students. He encouraged his son Kisshomaru and many of his leading students to study *Kashima Shinto Ryu kenjutsu*, as an adjunct to their training. Over many years of thought and training he devised a body of techniques where sword is used against sword, and then matched with unarmed techniques following the same pattern of manoeuvre and entry, where *uke* is disarmed and thrown. These techniques are both a product and a development of sword practice, introducing that special element of *aiki* blending that is Ueshiba *O Sensei*'s unique contribution to the theory and practice of Japanese martial arts.

The technique that exemplifies the principles of swordsmanship in practice more than any other is *shihonage*, or four direction throw. It requires a subtlety of understanding and application that is a measure of ones progress in aikido.

### SHIHONAGE (FOUR DIRECTION THROW)
*Basic Principles*

*Shihonage* is a technique that exemplifies all the basic principles of aikido practice incorporating *irimi* (entering), *tenkan* (the rotating turn of the body) and the cutting down of the hands as if wielding the sword. It is a simple technique but difficult in application, as it requires precise and centred movement of the body. The basis of the technique is that by entering and twisting *uke*'s arm through his own centre, wheeling through 180º and folding *uke*'s wrist and arm back over his own shoulder, you cut down from above your head as if with a sword, to throw your opponent to the rear.

Katate dori shihonage

It is named four direction throw, because it allows *nage* to control *uke* by varying the degree of rotation in order to choose in which direction to throw him. Whether the technique is initiated as a result of a side blow to the head, or the seizing of your hands or shoulder from a kneeling or standing position, the basis of the technique is the same. *Shihonage* can be adapted to meet the circumstance and defeat the attack. It is a principle weapon in aikido's arsenal of self-defence technique.

### KATATE DORI SHIHONAGE: COMMENTARY

From *migi gyaku-hanmi*, *uke* grasps *nage*'s left wrist to pull him forward. *Nage* strikes with the back of his right fist to *uke*'s eyes, *metsubushi*, to distract his opponent. *Nage* then seizes *uke*'s right wrist, lowers his hips and drives forward on his right foot across *uke*'s centre, as if thrusting forward with the sword, to break *uke*'s balance. Taking a big step with his left foot, *nage* raises *uke*'s hand above his head. *Nage* pivots 180º on both feet, folding *uke*'s arm by taking his right wrist to his right shoulder. *Nage* takes a *tsugi-ashi*, sliding step, and cuts down with his weight forward to break *uke*'s balance to the rear, causing him to fall.

## HOW IS AIKIDO TO BE USED?

Many martial arts share ethical values that emphasise the avoidance of conflict and look to their disciplines to improve the mental and physical health of their participants. Yet aikido stakes a claim to be more than this. Morihei Ueshiba not only believed that the philosophy of aikido should be non-violent but that this should be reflected in the technical process of aikido as a martial art itself. Painstakingly and with singular vision he fashioned the means by which an opponent's movement and mind can be 'read', interpreted and led into a technique where it can be neutralised. *Aiki* technique is the compassionate mind expressed in compassionate action.

# THE PARTING OF THE WAY: WAYS WITHIN THE WAY

## THE WAY GOES ON

Since the death of the Founder, Morihei Ueshiba *Sensei*, the legacy of aikido has passed to his son Kisshomaru Ueshiba *Sensei*, who is the current *Doshu* (Way Leader) of the *Aikikai* Foundation. It is the largest and most influential school of aikido with its legitimacy founded on the bedrock of the *Aikikai Hombu* (Head) *Dojo* itself; the founder's own *dojo* which still burns brightly with his influence.

The *Aikikai* is an international organisation with thousands of adherents throughout the world, affiliated through their clubs and associations to the *Hombu* and the living tradition it represents. Kisshomaru has managed to preserve this tradition by systemising the teaching of techniques, reducing the number practised to manageable proportions and by introducing carefully constructed grading programmes to guide the student's progress. The technical character of the tradition is represented in Kisshomaru Ueshiba's own flowing and very circular rendering of his father's teaching, which reflects *O Sensei*'s approach in his later years.

Kisshomaru Ueshiba, while still a young economics student at Waseda University, became Director of the *Kobukan Dojo* in 1942, upon his father's retirement to Iwama. It was undoubtedly the dedicated efforts of Kisshomaru Ueshiba that rescued aikido after World War II and built it into a modern *budo* with an international following. His visits to Europe, America and Australasia, together with his many books translated into the world's major languages, helped popularise the art and confirm his standing as *Doshu*. His son Moriteru, is *Dojo Cho* (chief instructor) of the *Aikikai Hombu*, and is the *Wakasensei*, or the 'young master' who is expected to lead the organisation in his own turn, as *Doshu*.

## THE WAY BROADENS

Within *Hombu* tradition there is a diversity of approach that does not always coincide with current practice at the *Aikikai Hombu* itself. Senior teachers, who were once *O Sensei*'s *deshi*, have their own legitimate visions of the Founder's teachings. These teachers either remain within the organisation or maintain a loose affiliation, but interpret aikido independently of the *Hombu*'s technical guidance.

One of these teachers, Morihiro Saito *Sensei*, 8th Dan, has developed a popular following for the equal emphasis that he places on training with weapons; these being the *jo* (wooden staff), *bokken* (sword) and *tanto* (knife). There is a stronger *budo* element to training, when students learn how to counter, or to use weapons in tandem with unarmed versions of the same techniques. Each unarmed throw, is matched by its equivalent technique using the *bokken* or *jo*. Saito *Sensei* believes that it is not possible to understand how the principles of swordsmanship form the basis of aikido technique, until you have trained consistently with a sword.

This is not a view shared by every senior teacher and it has provided some controversy in aikido circles. The alternative view stresses that any heavy emphasis on weapon training is inappropriate to our civilized times and compromises aikido's spiritual status as a non-aggressive martial way. Both views have their merits and both interpretations will be followed enthusiastically by aikido students. Saito *Sensei*'s authority in the aikido world is founded on his standing as Ueshiba *Sensei*'s longest serving and most devoted *deshi* (personal student). He was first taught by Ueshiba *Sensei* at his *budo* farm in Iwama in the summer of 1946. Ueshiba taught and farmed at Iwama throughout World War II, until the Hombu returned to Tokyo around 1956. He assisted *O Sensei* in constructing and founding the *Aiki* Shrine in Iwama, a place of great significance to *aikidoka* throughout the world. Today, he is acknowledged as the Shrine's Guardian and continues to teach at the *Ibaragi Dojo* in Iwama, on land he inherited from *O Sensei*. Many *aikidoka* from Europe and America visit Iwama to study with Saito *Sensei*, attracted by his desire to preserve and represent the full extent of Ueshiba *Sensei*'s aikido.

## THE WAY PARTS

Throughout this book we have described aikido according to its core principles, both in terms of philosophy and the mechanics of practice. This is the mainstream path of aikido represented in the Ueshiba family tradition and passed down to his son Kisshomaru Ueshiba and his grandson Moriteru Ueshiba. However, although the great majority of the clubs and *dojo* around the world will be practising within this mainstream tradition, it can no longer be said that there is only one aikido. Since the death of the Founder, Morihei Ueshiba, the organisational and ideological unity of *O Sensei*'s legacy has fragmented into several different groupings representing a variety of interpretations and aims. These aims range from a concern for spiritual discipline and idealism through self-defence, health and physical education to recreation

and sport. While each interpretation seeks broadly the same destination, each is convinced that they have found a slightly better way to get there.

Unlike karate, where a similarly diverse pattern exists, these schools all represent transformations of the teachings of one man, Morihei Ueshiba, by individuals who were directly taught by him, as trusted *deshi*, or personal students. During *O Sensei*'s lifetime these students, although already embarked on experimentation within the practice of aikido that would lead them in different directions, remained essentially loyal to their teacher and his organisation. Upon Ueshiba *Sensei*'s death however, circumstances changed and a few prominent disciples who wished to pursue their distinct interpretation of aikido, felt in good conscience that they should do so.

This diversity of practice can partly be explained by examining Ueshiba's career at the point at which each of these prominent *deshi* came into contact with him. In a career extending from the 1920s until his death in 1969, he taught many students, representing different generations. They learned from him at the different stages of his life, when his emphasis on the character of his art differed significantly. This ranged from the fierce self-defence orientated *aiki jujutsu* practice of his early days, through to the flowing circular forms of his latter years, when he was attempting physically to represent the concept of *budo* as 'love'. As Shirata *Sensei*, himself a prominent disciple of Morihei Ueshiba observed, 'within each generation each student had his or her own interpretation reflecting individual levels of progress, attitude and extent of spiritual insight'.

Although as time goes on the natural process of evolution will lead to the proliferation of more transformations of Ueshiba's work, as of this moment we need only recognise three alternative interpretations of aikido, that have established significant followings.

# YOSHINKAN AIKIDO

Founded by Gozo Shioda *Sensei* (*1915–1997*), a prominent pre-World War II student of Ueshiba *Sensei* and the first to forge a separate path from Ueshiba's own organisation. Its distinctness can be seen in its training methods and technical interpretation, rather than any difference of philosophy. This style has many associations with the Japanese military and police and is taught both to the Tokyo Riot Police, and to female police personnel. Although different, the *Yoshinkan* has always maintained good relations with the Ueshiba family tradition.

## TOMIKI AIKIDO OR AIKIDO KYOGI (SPORT AIKIDO)

Founded by Professor Kenji Tomiki (*1900–1981*) of Waseda University, which as its Japanese name implies is orientated towards sports practice and has established an entrenched position in the highly competitive environment of the Japanese University system. Tomiki was the most senior of Ueshiba's students to have founded his own style, bringing together aikido techniques with the *randori* (free-style) teaching methodologies familiar to judo. *Tomiki Aikido* organises and conducts international tournaments, attracting many competitors from across the globe as a regular feature of its international sporting programme.

## SHIN SHIN TOITSU AIKIDO

Founded by Koichi Tohei (*1920-* ), who was at one time aikido's favourite 'son' and leading exponent of the orthodox tradition. His insistence that the development of *ki* can easily be generated through specific exercises rather than waited for as the outcome of long practice, brought him into ideological dispute with the *Aikikai* and led him to found his own school of aikido. Tohei's school is primarily concerned with harnessing *ki*, to be used in our daily lives to promote health and mental vitality.

Each of these schools offers a different answer to the question 'what is aikido?' Although from *dojo* to *dojo*, you will see the same techniques, etiquette and broad philosophical perspective, the differences are important and address the question, 'what kind of aikido will suit me?' We will examine each of these styles in the next three chapters, to provide a fuller picture of the range and variety of aikido practice that Ueshiba *Sensei*'s inheritance represents.

Choice, however, might not be open to you, as the local *dojo* will represent only one style of aikido and there may be no convenient alternative. In this case you can be confident that if you are interested in practising aikido, all versions are sufficiently alike to provide a stimulating and meaningful experience. However, if you have options then it would be as well to consider the differences to see how comfortable you feel with the alternative styles of practice. Remember that although this may help you make an initial choice, you may not appreciate what it is that you want from aikido until you have experienced it for yourself.

# THE MARTIAL WAY: GOZO SHIODA AND THE YOSHINKAN

ozo Shioda, the 'little giant' of aikido, named for his diminutive height and formidable technical ability, was one of the most outstanding teachers of aikido, living or dead. Anyone who had the privilege of seeing him in action effortlessly flooring *ukes* at least twice his size, with the precision and timing of true mastery, could not fail to witness the graceful power of aikido.

Shioda, like so many other masters of aikido, began his *budo* training as a youth with judo and kendo, finally discovering aikido as a young university student. He entered the *Kobukan Dojo* in Tokyo in 1932, where he studied for eight years with Ueshiba *Sensei*, until World War II interrupted his training. Following service in the military he resumed training after the war, spending a brief period at Iwama, the present day location of the *Aiki* Shrine.

After the war when the martial arts lay under the ban of the Allied Occupation authorities, great efforts were made by many teachers to redefine and reorganise the martial ways to eschew the ultra-nationalist image and represent themselves in a new acceptable form for Japan's emerging civil society. In 1954, an exhibition of the martial ways took place in Tokyo, under the auspices of the Life Extension Society. Shioda *Sensei* took part in this event and his skilled performance attracted a great deal of favourable attention, so much so that aikido began to gain a great deal of popularity. A group of financiers, witnessing this development, decided to back Shioda in the foundation of the *Yoshinkan Dojo* in Tokyo, with Shoshiro Kudo as president and Gozo Shioda as the *Dojo* chief.

Shioda's style of aikido is what he considered to be a faithful rendering of the pre-war *Aiki Budo* techniques which he learned first hand from Ueshiba, then at his technical peak. They are therefore much more combat orientated than some modern aikido styles, although the spiritual goals of aikido remain in tune with those of the *Aikikai*. Indeed separation from the *Aikikai*, was a gradual process, not the product of an acute ideological rift.

The *Yoshinkan*, named from a previous *dojo* run by Shioda's father, has become one of the largest aikido organisations with branches throughout the world. *Yoshinkan's* vigorous use of *atemi* and combat orientated technique has recommended itself to many Japanese police forces, particularly in Tokyo, where many police officers spend time training with *Yoshinkan* instructors.

Shioda *Sensei*, a man of unique personal spirit who electrified the atmosphere whenever he walked out onto the mats, died in 1994. Small in stature but great of heart, he lived the true *budo* life.

Shioda *Sensei's* legacy has been inherited by his son Yasuhiro Shioda (b. 1952), who began his daily training in aikido at the *Yoshinkan Hombu Dojo* at the age of thirteen. After graduating from Chuo University with a Degree in Economics, he taught aikido to police departments and to university clubs throughout Japan.

In 1984 Yasuhiro Shioda came to the UK, spending three years in England where he was able to create the basis for *Yoshinkan Aikido's* expansion to the West. This expansion continues world wide through the efforts of the International *Yoshinkan* Aikido Federation, which recognises *Yoshinkan* groups and organisations and assists them to maintain contact with the centre, preserve standards and raise the profile and popularity of the style.

## YOSHINKAN AIKIDO:
## THE PHILOSOPHY OF PRACTICE

Of all the major styles of aikido to emerge from the teachings of Morihei Ueshiba, Gozo Shioda's *Yoshinkan* remains closest to its pre-World War II technical roots. When Shioda became a student of Ueshiba *Sensei*, aikido was still in its formative stages and was then called *Aiki Budo*. The character of the techniques and the manner of their execution still bore the marks of the *Daito Ryu Aiki jujutsu* curriculum which *O Sensei* had learnt from his own master, Sokaku Takeda. This was a forceful, martial style of *aiki jujutsu*, concerned primarily with the efficiency and effectiveness of technique in combat. Practice at that time reflected this spirit and was hard, fast and relentless. Shioda *Sensei* revelled in this form of practice and it undoubtedly influenced the nature of the training methods he put in place at his own school, the *Yoshinkan*, after World War II.

Post World War II Japan was a nation in social turmoil as it sought to get a grip on the new economic and political realities, precipitated by the Allied Powers' occupation. Strikes and unrest required security and police organisations to find methods of self-defence that would be non-brutal, effective and still meet the restraints expected by Japan's new democratic society. This was the milieu in which Shioda *Sensei* began to operate. Between 1952 and 1953 Shioda *Sensei* visited eighty three police stations giving aikido demonstrations. His success in attracting the interest of security forces was served by his willingness to take on all comers and his ability to throw the largest of experienced police *judoka* with unexpected ease.

These demonstrations forged a lasting association with the Tokyo Metropolitan Police Department, and to this day, all policewomen receive instruction in aikido, under the tutelage of Kyoichi Inoue, one of the *Yoshinkan*'s most respected senior teachers. Each year ten students are also selected from Tokyo's Police Riot Squad, to train intensively in aikido and are put through a vigorous and gruelling black belt instructors' programme. While it is not strictly a requirement for all officers to undergo aikido training, a *kyu* grade is expected of officers wishing to take the qualifying test for police sergeant.

As one can see, the *Yoshinkan* has responded to the needs of police officers who will have to use aikido techniques in action on Tokyo's streets. This sense of practical reality and combat effectiveness pervades the whole of the *Yoshinkan* curriculum.

Differences that exist between the *Aikikai* and the *Yoshinkan* are largely matters of technical interpretation, not philosophical dispute. This has enabled the *Yoshinkan* to maintain its distinctive approach yet still enjoy good relations with the *Aikikai* mainstream. However, the essential technical pragmatism Shioda demonstrated throughout his teaching, may be said to have coloured his view of what actually constitutes *ki* and how we obtain it.

## THE QUESTION OF KI

In an interview he gave to the journal *Aiki News*, published in 1993, Shioda castigated modern aikido as being 'dimensionless' and 'empty of content'. He believed that many students were only imitating the 'outside' of the technique and had not sufficiently 'paid their dues'. This had led many into believing that if they imitated the soft flowing aikido, characteristic of *O Sensei* and many of the teachers who had been with Ueshiba in the early days, they too would have the same power. Shioda declared this to be a grave error. All of his generation who studied with Ueshiba *Sensei* before the War, were young, fit and tough and had arrived at his *dojo* with previous experience of judo, *jujutsu* or kendo. Ueshiba exhorted them to use all their strength and power, Shioda observed, as 'only O *Sensei* was able to perform techniques without resorting to power'.

Shioda *Sensei* believed that the way to finding *aiki* was to go through a necessary process of several developmental stages, none of which could be skipped. In the early stages, Shioda said, 'you must use every bit of your power and exert yourself in training'. However much you are told not to use power or force, as a beginner you will be unable to comply. Gradually over the course of time your body will begin to absorb the lessons of practice and be able to judge instinctively the precise force required; this is *aiki*.

*Ki*, as it is manifested in aikido is the conjunction of its basic components; correct posture, maintaining centre, breathing, timing and focused power, which together put us into perfect balance. To be able to summon *ki*, by Shioda's definition, is therefore to have 'the mastery of balance'. Harmonizing your *ki* with another, is therefore a question of developing sensitivities to your partner's speed, timing and power. Eventually training will bring you to a point where you will be able to 'read' the intentions of your opponent, to know when he is going to attack and to be aware of the direction the attack will come from, almost before it is launched. Shioda has described this as a 'see/feel energy' and gaining it is seen as the major purpose of training.

Spiritually, to harmonize with the universe is to be in balance, body and mind. *Aiki*, the harmonizing of energy is the manifestation of this balance and requires you to let go of your own ego and follow the natural rhythm of the universe. It is a technique of spiritual non-resistance.

When first witnessing a *Yoshinkan Aikido* training session, the observer may be struck by the low, deep stances and strong, angular movements that bear an outside resemblance to karate. Students form lines and perform solo exercises to the commands of the *sensei*, in complex *kata*-like patterns of hand and body movements. Similarly techniques are often introduced and taught with the whole class as a unit, each student mirroring the steps taken by the *sensei* and his *uke* simultaneously.

Old film sequences of the *Yoshinkan's* early days in the 1950s show shots of two instructors mounted on a podium, while around them scores of police cadets perform the techniques in step by step synchronicity. As a secure and logical learning process, with all the benefits of drill, it is a solid base upon which freer expressions of aikido can be laid.

## HOW THE TRAINING SYSTEM IS ORGANISED

### KIHON DOSA, OR BASIC MOVEMENTS

The *Kihon Dosa*, or basic movements form the foundation upon which the style is constructed. To perform *Kihon Dosa* and to keep the shape and purpose of these movements in the performance of technique, is the essence of *Yoshinkan Aikido*. These six basic movements, grouped in sets of two, teach the use of *hiriki no yosei*, or elbow power; *tai no henko*, or body change movement and in the two *shumatsu dosa*, or after class exercises, the stretching of the body and harmonization with a partner's energy.

Beginners learn to perform entering and turning movements and how to focus power through the body while keeping a stable posture. In the early stages of learning, these exercises are performed solo, before and after the main body of the lesson. More advanced *aikidoka* perform these exercises with a partner to develop an awareness of where to exploit the partner's weak line, develop breath power and connect with the outflow of their energy. Advanced students may also practice these exercises with a *bokken*, the wooden training sword.

## KIHON WAZA, OR BASIC TECHNIQUES

*Kihon Waza*, or basic techniques are organised on familiar aikido lines into:

- *Suwari waza*, when two partners, named *sh'te* (defender) and *uke* (attacker), face each other in the kneeling, or *seiza* position.
- *Hanmi handachi waza*, with *sh'te* kneeling and *uke* standing.
- *Tachi waza*, where both partners are standing.
- *Ushiro waza*, where *uke* attacks *sh'te* from behind.

At this level techniques are carried out in the characteristic *Yoshinkan* manner, which separates out each movement to be performed individually, step by step. *Sh'te* and *uke*, approach each other in a precise stylised manner, maintaining a very formal guard and posture, or *kamae*. *Uke* delivers the formal attack but makes no attempt deliberately to unbalance or oppose *sh'te*, allowing the opportunity for *sh'te* systematically to drill the techniques into the body and the subconscious mind.

## APPLIED TECHNIQUES

Applied techniques have developed from the foundation of *kihon waza*, and are performed in one seamless movement. At this stage of training the student begins to put together all the elements of speed, reaction and manoeuvre, necessary to skilled self-defence. Applied techniques are also performed against weapons such as the *bokken* (sword), *tanto* (knife) and *jo* (staff).

In order to develop and practise advanced skills and provide a sense of combat reality, free-style techniques are used against continuous but prescribed attacks. *Uke* will attack *sh'te* with an overhead strike or by grasping his hand or any number of agreed attacks, with *sh'te* responding to the assault with a spontaneous choice of technique. Each time *uke* is thrown he or she will take a breakfall, rise, and attack *sh'te* again until 'time' is called on the exercise. This exercise can be extended to meet multiple attackers, where you may experiment against two or three opponents, attacking empty handed or with a combination of weapons.

## THE SENIOR LEVELS OF TRAINING

At the higher levels of training, students receive instruction in the most difficult of all skills; how to unbalance an opponent who has locked out their body with the deliberate aim of thwarting you. At the highest of levels the *ogi*, or hidden techniques, demonstrate a mastery of aikido's myriad subtleties.

# THE IMPORTANCE OF ATEMI

The founder Ueshiba *Sensei* placed great emphasis on *atemi* in combat, maintaining that in 'a real battle, *atemi* is seventy percent, technique is thirty percent.' True to its distinctive *aiki jujutsu* character, a feature of training within the *Yoshinkan* is the systematic employment of *atemi* in the execution of aikido technique.

As we have explained above, *atemi* are strikes or blows delivered against physiological weak points. These strikes are made with the tips of the fingers, side of the hand, elbow, knee, toes or the heels. However the form of strike most frequently used in *Yoshinkan Aikido* is *metsubushi*, the 'smashing of the eyes' blow, which is made by striking the point directly between the eyes, with the knuckle at the base of the middle finger.

Whenever *sh'te* is seized or grasped by *uke*, a *metsubushi* strike is made to *uke*'s eyes. The purpose of the blow is to 'blind', distract, and destabilize the opponent, creating an opportunity for *sh'te* to execute a technique. Within the *Yoshinkan*, the *metsubushi* is carried out with a practised determination and is met instantly by a block from *uke*, made with the open palm raised in front of the face to protect the eyes. This gives *sh'te* the opportunity to strike habitually and instinctively towards the eyes and for uke to practise speedy and responsive blocking tactics, without anyone getting hurt.

Techniques taken to the ground, where *uke* is pinned down on the back and controlled by *sh'te* using one hand, are also likely to be finished with a *tegatana* (sword-hand) strike made with the free hand to *uke*'s head. Further strikes can be made against pressure points, using the second knuckle of the first or second finger. Again, the intention is to distract the opponent long enough for a hold to be secured and the technique carried through.

Of course, as we described in Chapter 4, *atemi* is also a matter of exploiting an opponent's loss of balance to throw him down. If we time the moment we may be able to use any part of the body, such as the back, chest or forearm, through which to focus energy and throw *uke* down.

## THE CHARACTER OF A YOSHINKAN AIKIDO DOJO

In matters of *dojo* etiquette, before, during and after the training element of a lesson, *Yoshinkan* practice would be familiar to any traditional *aikidoka*. Ritual claps and bows are made from the *seiza* position facing a modest *aiki* shrine accompanied by pictures of Shioda *Sensei* and Ueshiba *Sensei*. After these observances are made and the practice begins, a visitor from another style of aikido would detect a more 'martial' character to the conduct of *dojo* discipline.

This martial character does not prevent the *Yoshinkan dojo* from being a place where the atmosphere is relaxed and the *aikidoka* friendly. There is also laughter and the sheer exuberant joy of practice, but the path to attaining these benefits are seen as best served through a very formal discipline. The *Yoshinkan* has maintained a very traditional Japanese interpretation of discipline and etiquette, which has survived its transfer to the West.

This is not a martial culture for the sloppy or the unkempt, however you may choose to present yourself outside the *dojo*. A potentially dangerous martial art, such as aikido, particularly a version of aikido that maintains an emphasis on the reality and effectiveness of technique, requires an alert attentive mind that does not wander from the matter in hand.

The commands of the *sensei* must be strictly observed in your whole person, without hesitation or reluctance to demonstrate the seriousness with which you are approaching training. Therefore, a traditionally inspired *dojo* of this kind would expect instructions from the *sensei* to be carried out immediately, particularly when taking up formal positions on the *dojo* floor.

Great emphasis is placed on training the beginner to understand the codes of behaviour expected in the *dojo* and how they should be carried out with the required pace and form. This sets a foundation for the beginner's training, signalling their willingness and enthusiasm to learn and to discipline their span of attention. It is a humane, but formally tough regime that appeals particularly to those seeking to follow a stricter path of self-discipline. As we have seen, this is not to say that other styles of aikido are not strict or even formal, but in the degree to which this is observed in presentation and manner,

the *Yoshinkan* must be considered the most orthodox of all the major styles.

For training all *aikidoka* wear the white *keikogi*, or training suit, with *kyu* ranks distinguished in the West by the wearing of a variety of coloured belts. Dan grades do wear the traditional black *hakama*, but normally this is reserved for more formal occasions. For the regular lesson, unless they are of the highest rank, they will be seen in *keikogi*, tied round with familiar black belt.

Once a year the All Japan *Yoshinkai Aikido* Demonstration is held to celebrate another year in the *Yoshinkan's* annual calendar. This is an opportunity to bring members of the *Yoshinkan* together to witness and be inspired by demonstrations given by leading exponents of the style. They also have an opportunity to participate themselves, by taking part in a demonstration event open to all *Yoshinkan* clubs. Teams from competing clubs present formal routines, demonstrating different aspects of aikido skills, before a panel of senior teachers who will judge their performances and establish a winner and runners up. These routines are very varied and seek to demonstrate the strength and unity of the *dojo*, rather than highlight individual skills. Of course skill, the conduct of the team, their togetherness and the continuity of the performance, are highly important in making judgements, but so is spirit. Teams may comprise *kyu* grades as easily as black belts, or may mix both. For this is a competition to witness pride in the *dojo* and in the aikido you practise. As *Yoshinkan Aikido* has expanded across the world, events of this kind, sometimes international in composition, are being staged outside of Japan providing a celebration of the *Yoshinkan's* achievements to a broader stage.

Despite the formality and the discipline, women are well represented in the style and are not put off by its 'toughness'. We have noted that all Tokyo Metropolitan policewomen receive aikido training under the supervision of Inoue *Sensei*, who has made it his passionate concern to ensure that this training will be effective in their self defence. Recently, he has experimented with a form of free practice, to encourage them to sustain skills and timing when faced with unyielding competitive pressure from an opponent within a framework of rules.

Women have also participated in the notorious 'instructor's course'; a year of intensive aikido training and study that may bring you from beginner to black belt, make you a good *Yoshinkan* coach, or break you! This course is strictly for the determined and requires total immersion into a very ordered Japanese *budo* culture, which insists on disciplines many Westerners find hard to understand. This instructor's course was once held alongside that of the Riot Squad and all students were expected to make the same commitment to the intensity of training expected of a disciplined force.

Men and women from both Japan and other parts of the world have gone through this training and emerged with solid technical skills and practical coaching experience. This ability to send out an annual core of teachers, who have met the exacting requirements set by the *Yoshinkan*'s most senior teachers, has undoubtedly ensured that the high standards of *Yoshinkan Hombu* style coaching permeates the *Yoshinkan dojo*. If you are fit and have the means to support yourself in Japan, together with mental resilience and strong spirit, then the instructor's course might be for you. The course provides a unique fast track introduction to a core understanding of *Yoshinkan Aikido* that would take many more years to discover in a weekly cycle of two or three classes.

The unique contribution that Shioda *Sensei* made to the growth and development of aikido was not to innovate or to change the purpose of the techniques he learned at first hand from the Founder. Rather it was to preserve what he learned in

the famous *Jigoku Dojo* (Hell Dojo) and ensure its survival into modern times. The *Yoshinkan* remains true to this tradition and provides an aikido with dynamic realism well suited to the needs of self protection and the discipline of the spirit.

# 7

# THE SPORTING WAY: KENJI TOMIKI AND TOMIKI AIKIDO

Of all the currents represented in the new styles of aikido which have developed since the death of the Founder, Morihei Ueshiba, Kenji Tomiki's seems to have travelled furthest from the source. Far from discouraging competition, Tomiki and his followers have adopted a form of aikido that can be contested in the sports arena, with the full panoply of players, officials and spectators cheering on their team.

For the *Doshu*, Kisshomaru Ueshiba, and the senior teachers who have continued to follow the *Aikikai Hombu* tradition, a competitive aikido system contradicts the Founder's central philosophy of 'harmony with the spirit'. The competitive nature of sport seems an unlikely means of reconciling conflict and promoting spiritual insight and personal growth. Yet, despite this heretical exterior, *Tomiki Aikido* claims both a technical and a spiritual allegiance to Morihei Ueshiba's original teachings.

## KENJI TOMIKI: THE FOUNDER OF TOMIKI AIKIDO

Kenji Tomiki began his study of *budo* at the age of ten with Kano's *Kodokan Judo*. He studied under Kano at his *Kodokan dojo* while a student of Waseda University in Tokyo. Throughout his life he retained an active association with judo, rising to the rank of 9th Dan. He entered Ueshiba's *dojo* in 1925 and became one of Ueshiba's most prominent disciples; a relationship that was encouraged by Dr Kano.

Tomiki went to Manchuria in 1936, as an instructor at the *Daido Gakuin* and then at Kenkoku University which opened in 1938. At Kenkoku he established an *Aiki Budo* course which featured as a regular part of the curriculum, a project aided by his close associate Hideo Ohba. After the war and internment in a Russian POW camp, he returned to Japan and worked at the *Kodokan*, the judo headquarters, where he campaigned for the lifting of the ban imposed on the martial arts by the American occupation authorities.

In 1953 he established an aikido club at Waseda University and aikido became a regular element of the curriculum. However an important proviso placed on this development by the University authorities was that it should have a competitive element. Accordingly, during his years as a professor of physical education at the university, he developed a competitive format for aikido based on judo principles of *randori*.

It was Tomiki *Sensei*'s long term intention of having aikido accepted, alongside judo and kendo, into the Japanese school and university system, as the third national educational *budo*. National and international competition are also important aspirations which are served by annual national championships and by major biennial international *Tomiki Aikido* tournaments.

Although he still taught aikido at Ueshiba's *Aikikai Hombu* until the early 1960s, it was clear that Tomiki's development of a sport aikido was not welcome, and a gradual distancing took place. Despite this disapproval Tomiki remained loyal to Ueshiba *Sensei* until his death in 1969.

1970, the year of his retirement as Professor of Physical Education, saw the culmination of his efforts, when the First All Japan University Aikido Championships were held at Okubo Sports Centre, in Tokyo. From that point on a break was inevitable and, in 1974, the All Japan Aikido Association was set up to administer and develop *Aikido Kyogi*, or Sport Aikido, with Professor Tomiki as its first Chairman.

*Tomiki Aikido* has also expanded to the West, particularly Britain, the USA and Australia where it has significant followings. This has enabled it to stage international championships on a four yearly cycle, beginning with the First International Open *Aikido* Tournament, at Tenri University in 1989. This event was attended by over 200 competitors from nine countries. In 1997 there was an even larger event staged in Imabari on the island of Shikoku, which received first day news coverage from the Japanese public television network NHK, and was attended by an ex-prime minister and sponsored by a major soft drinks company.

Although *Tomiki Aikido* has not managed to overtake the traditional path pursued by the *Aikikai Hombu*, either in membership or international profile, it is a significant force appealing particularly to the young and those who enjoy the excitement of competition.

# TOMIKI AIKIDO: THE PHILOSOPHY OF PRACTICE

*Tomiki Aikido* is based on the principle that the most effective way to preserve the best of the traditional values and moral systems represented in classical Japanese *budo*, or martial ways, is to convert them into sports. In this way the martial arts can be made accessible to modern civil societies, where the ruthless dedication of the *Samurai* to the arts of war, is completely inappropriate.

# WHAT IS TOMIKI AIKIDO?

*Tomiki Aikido* has been defined as a blend of:

- physical education
- sport
- self-defence

## AIKIDO AS PHYSICAL EDUCATION

Tomiki, in his book *Discussions on Budo* recognised two important perspectives for the pursuit of aikido as modern physical education:

> 'Firstly, it is the means by which one maintains good health, through physical activity which involves the whole body, and increases physical strength.'

> 'Secondly, a spiritual dimension is achievable as a result of physical activity. In other words, through diligence in exercise and sports, free will is disciplined, self-assertiveness is encouraged, importance is attached to respect, and a temperate, conciliatory nature is forged.'

## AIKIDO AS SPORT

Professor Tomiki suggested that modern international ideals of sportsmanship and humane behaviour, promoted through the discipline of sport, equate to the traditional Japanese practice of *gyo*, or spiritual exercise. *Gyo* is physical activity, not introspective meditation and is the means to 'train the heart and discipline the spirit'. Without a context in which to cultivate the heart it is like 'learning to swim on *tatami* mats'.

Tomiki argued that the *Samurai* had created *budo* as a spiritual exercise, to help them come to terms with the constant possibility

of death in combat. The exercises in the *dojo* were given ever present meaning by the dangers faced outside its walls in armed encounters and war. Tomiki observed that it was both unrealistic and undesirable in an open society to practice in this classical *budo* tradition of 'training to walk with death', yet there must still be a way in which we can test our courage, determination and skill. If techniques are only ever learnt formally in agreed patterns with cooperative partners, then there is every likelihood that over the years they will become misinterpreted, altered, and devoid of effectiveness.

He believed that the sports arena could provide an effective substitute for the arena of war, and be acceptable to a peaceful civil society. The benefits accrued by the *Samurai* in training for war must now be obtained by training for competition.

Technical skills are encouraged by the wish to go higher, faster and be stronger, and are tested in a situation of stressful unpredictability. The use of *shiai*, or contest, is therefore the most effective way to keep skills alive and effective. Even if they are constrained by rules, they have true meaning in that they fit their purpose.

Spiritual training is reinterpreted as the cultivation of sportsmanship. It is the test of character and determination to win, but *not* at all costs. You must play to win, but fairly, with humanity, dignity and courteous concern for your opponent. Put simply, it is the code of the *Samurai* recast in the ideals of Olympian sportsmanship. Therefore, Tomiki said, 'the spiritual training, or *seishin*, of sport, is not about winning, but competing courageously'. These are the qualities of *Tomiki Aikido*, which through international competition seeks in a modest way to establish friendships and promote cultural exchange across the boundaries of nation states.

To summarize, the purpose of *aikido* sports competition is to:

- Provide an incentive to train consistently and perfect skills.
- Provide a context where techniques are tested to see if they really work.
- Promote development and experimentation if they do not.
- Train the heart and discipline the spirit.
- Bring together *aikidoka* from across the world in open competition.
- Foster international friendship and world peace.

## AIKIDO AS SELF-DEFENCE

While it is difficult to eradicate violence from our streets there will remain a legitimate reason for acquiring the skills of self-defence. *Tomiki Aikido* provides for this training through two extended sequences of grouped techniques, or *kata*. These are known as the *Goshin No Kata*, or *kata* of self-defence (alternatively the *Koryu Dai San No Kata*), which involves defences against strikes and attacks with weapons, and the *Goshin Ho*, which includes defences against kicks.

Training for sports competition, through *randori* (or free/open practice), provides the opportunity to acquire the skills of timing, tactical thinking and commitment to technique that build confidence in dealing with real aggression.

The concept of self-defence however, is much more broadly drawn than a simple concern for self-protection. Tomiki saw self-defence as also being concerned with more general aspects of safety, such as the maintenance of our own health and well-being through the physical education aikido provides. Self-defence should also include a concern for others and a preparation for human crises and natural disasters. Aikido helps us to acquire the mental health and human resilience required to face the ordinary and extraordinary challenges of life.

Self-defence means, therefore:

- Keeping the body fit and healthy.
- Developing the mental strength to respond to danger and stress.
- Acquiring the skills to protect yourself and others, effectively and safely.

## HOW IS TOMIKI AIKIDO TAUGHT?

The curriculum of *Tomiki Aikido* is arguably the most systematic and physical education-orientated of all the major styles of aikido. Its approach is essentially modular and designed to introduce basic skills, exercises designed to promote the mobility of these skills, and a level of fitness that can sustain clear actions under pressure.

Basic exercises teach the principles of breaking an opponent's balance, timing and how to exploit combinations of techniques. Particular attention is placed on developing the skills of *taisabaki*, or the manoeuvring of the body to both evade attack and set yourself up (*tsukuri*) for countering with an aikido technique. To this extent all learning is ultimately orientated towards being able to use aikido skills naturally in any circumstances.

This emphasis on what is natural, is the starting point for the practise of all technique. To emphasize this point, Professor Tomiki sometimes conducted his lectures and demonstrations of aikido in business suit, shirt and tie. Thus all *Tomiki Aikido* techniques begin in *shizentai*, or natural posture with hands by the side and the feet placed directly beneath the shoulders. No *kamae* or defensive posture is taken up until the attack is fully committed, simulating a situation of surprise. Although this has important self-defence spin-offs, its purpose is to develop the marriage of ready mind and speed of reaction that are the essential ingredients of sports competition.

The traditional description of this state is *mushin*, or 'no-mind', which finds physical expression in *mugamae*, or 'no-posture', the ultimate goal of true *budo*. We must remind ourselves that *Tomiki Aikido* is a modern *budo* with the characteristics of sport, but that unlike Western sports, it retains aims that extend beyond technical excellence or physical performance. It is a spiritual aim, rooted in the belief that the body can often serve the spirit, more ably than the intellect.

*Mushin* (no-mind-ness) is this spiritual state which has been described by Donn Draeger, the eminent *budo* historian, as a condition where the mind 'negates itself, lets go from itself, and divests itself of all dualistic concepts about this and that – good and bad, right and wrong, gain and loss, life and death – all of which must be seen as a oneness.' *Mushin* is a mind not disturbed by effects of any kind, the corollary of which is *mugamae* (no-posture-ness), where the body takes no position or physical attitude of expectation to signal an intention. *Mushin mugamae*, therefore, makes possible the skilful performance of technique without any 'conscious efforts made to generate and sustain it'. It is the state that modern Western sports personalities are beginning to describe as the *zone*, where a state of acute mental alertness and meditative calm slows time and transforms one's performance into record breaking achievement.

To develop this ability, *Tomiki Aikido* is taught through two processes adapted from judo; the learning of techniques through *kata*, and the free practice of these techniques in *randori*.

## KATA

While all aikido is technically *kata budo*, or the practice of technique as a prearranged sequence of movement, *Tomiki Aikido*'s approach to *kata* is different from the other styles. Techniques are not just taught individually on a stand-alone basis, but are grouped into sets of techniques or variations of technique, that demonstrate a common principle or theme.

The most important of these sets of technique is called the *Junanahon*, or more formally, the *Randori no Kata*. As its name suggests, it is a group of seventeen techniques which form the basis for the practice of *randori shiai*, or 'free-play' competition. The *Randori no Kata*, together with its partner, the *Ura no Kata*, which demonstrates how ten techniques from the *junanahon* can be used to counter ten others, forms the core of *Tomiki Aikido* competition technique. Through the repetitive practice of these forms in their distinct sets, the student is taught the principles of timing, evasive action and the breaking of an opponent's balance, which he will go on to use freely in the parallel practice of *randori*.

At each stage of their progress through the grades, the *Tomiki Aikido* student will perform parts, or all, of these sets sequentially, for examination, as it is considered the basic foundation of their technical repertoire. These basic techniques are simple and direct and begin from the point where two people walking directly towards each other come to a sudden confrontation, when one is attacked by the other. *Tori* then defeats *uke*, after which they move away and restart the process until a sequence of techniques is completed.

Throughout the performance of a *kata* both players must display a synchronicity of mind and movement, coordinating their timing and their awareness and sensitivity to each other's actions to perfect their *aikido* skills. It is much more a cooperative learning process designed to reveal the mind of *aikido*, than it is the process of learning techniques. Without confidence in one's partner and a developed understanding of each other's abilities, it will not be possible to fulfil the promise of the *kata*'s script and convey its meaning.

All the myriad techniques that make up the canon of aikido *waza*, which lie outside the practice of free-style competition,

are also taught through this sequential *kata* process. These are generally known as *koryu*, or traditional (classical) *waza*. The most important of these being the *Koryu Goshin no Kata*, a set of techniques that demonstrate aikido self-defence techniques, against a variety of attacks. This *kata* forms the backbone to understanding all the principles of aikido self-defence including good eye contact, spatial awareness, timing and the breaking of an opponents posture, against a variety of attacks, including grapples and strikes with hands and weapons. Each *kata* sequence presents different aspects of the problems encountered in self-defence situations and how aikido principles can solve them.

Buttressed around the *Randori*, *Ura* and *Goshin kata* are further sets of techniques, which construct the body of aikido systematically around the *Randori no Kata* core. The student is introduced to these *kata* forms at different stages of training, as their skills and awareness develop, fleshing out their knowledge of the applied principles of basic technique.

## EMBU

*Kata* is also a part of *Tomiki Aikido*'s competitive system, and these sequences of technique are performed in an event known as *embu*. Two partners, acting as *tori* and *uke* perform a *kata* within a timed period in front of a panel of judges. The judges award points for technical merit and understanding and interpretation of the *kata*'s meaning, much in the same way as an Olympic ice-skating competition is adjudicated.

There are basically two types of *kata* competition known as *kitei embu*, where the prescribed *kata* of *Tomiki Aikido* are demonstrated and *jiyu embu*, or free-style *embu*. In the free-style event, competitors are given the creative opportunity to devise their own sequences for performance. Once again, this is analogous to the set figures and free-style events of ice-skating.

*Embu* competition affords the incentive for *Tomiki Aikido* practitioners to focus their training and improve their aikido skills on an important temporary goal, in their long-term struggle for mastery. All students are encouraged to participate, as this helps to set standards across the style, to which all can compare and relate their own performance and teaching of technique. *Embu* therefore serves a dual purpose, providing a challenge for the participants and a means of checking the quality of teaching and interpretation in individual *dojo*.

*Kata embu*, has become increasingly popular as an event, as it does not require the levels of fitness and determination required for *randori* events. *Embu* gives expression to the ritual, the beauty, and the aesthetic of aikido and gives those who are too old or temperamentally disinclined to take part in *aikido randori* contests an important place in *Tomiki Aikido*'s cycle of events.

## RANDORI

*Randori* is the methodology of learning that distinguishes *Tomiki Aikido* from all other aikido schools. Although *randori*, as a free form of training, is practised in other styles at senior levels, only *Tomiki Aikido* seeks to teach it methodically from beginner to black belt and beyond.

Essentially *randori* is a process where the *aikidoka* takes 'freedom in action', facing an opponent who delivers a succession of random and unpredictable attacks against which the *aikidoka* must defend himself. The continuous flow of attacks prevents him from having the space to think of a technique appropriate to the moment. They must 'pop-out' of his head without conscious thought. This can only be learnt through training which makes the application of aikido skills instinctive. *Randori* training is the process by which this is done.

*Randori* training begins with a variety of drills designed to teach fast body evasion, blocks, counter moves and breaking

the balance of an opponent. This leads on to a hierarchy of different levels of *randori* skills and performance, which are practised inter-changeably by all students, irrespective of grade and experience, to rebuild their skills and prepare the mind. These are termed; *kakarigeiko, hikitategeiko, randorigeiko* and culminate with *shiai*, a competitive aikido match. In any one lesson, the student may progress through one or more of these successive exercises as a constant of the training programme.

Each of these exercises has its particular characteristics which are described below:

## KAKARIGEIKO

At the first level of *randori* practice, partners face each other across the mat; they give a standing bow and on the command of the *sensei* (teacher), they engage. One *aikidoka* acts as an attacker (*uke*), while the other acts as the defender (*tori*). For a specified time period (anything from a minute to a minute and a half), *tori* defends against *uke*'s attacks and attempts to control *uke* by throwing him to the ground or immobilizing him with a joint-locking technique.

*Tori* is able to apply freely any of the basic 17 techniques (*Junanahon*), the 10 counter-techniques (*ura-waza*) and their variations. *Tori*'s choice of technique is in direct response to the speed, direction and method of *uke*'s attacks and has not been predetermined.

*Uke* attempts to press home an attack on *tori*, by seizing him, throwing him to the floor with an *atemi* move or scoring a hit with a *tanto*, or training knife, made of pliable rubber and soft padding. A hit, or *tsukiari*, is made when any part of *tori*'s body above the waist and below the shoulders is convincingly struck by *uke*'s *tanto*. *Uke* can evade *tori*'s actions and techniques by movement and the correct use of posture, similar to those used in *kata*, but no actual resistance is made to *tori*'s application of technique once it is initiated.

At the end of the specified time period, the roles are reversed. *Kakarigeiko*, is controlled at all times by the *sensei*, who times the exercise and supervises its safety. Unarmed practice is termed *toshu kakarigeiko* and armed practice (with the training 'knife'), *tanto kakarigeiko*.

In *kakarigeiko*, or attack practice, the *aikidoka* is able to begin to learn how to apply all that has been learnt from *kata* and preparation exercises in a situation of controlled stress. Cooperation and safety are still the keynotes of the exercise. *Tori* will not throw *uke* to the floor gratuitously, or apply a lock severely. *Uke*, will not resist with all his strength and determination. It is light, quick practice where *uke* darts in unpredictably and *tori* evades and counters on the move, each player manoeuvring for tactical advantage.

In this stage of the *randori* process, *tori* is given the opportunity to practice technique in a context that begins to approximate to a real contest, without fear of injury or resistance. The *aikidoka* then begins to take the steps towards a creative interpretation of technique by learning how to adapt what she has learnt to suit actual circumstances, her own physical characteristics and level of fitness.

Good *randori* requires a reasonable level of fitness. *Randori* practice may constitute a quarter to a third of a *Tomiki Aikido* lesson, with several *kakarigeiko* or higher level bouts taking place. Each partner will have taken many breakfalls as *uke*, and both partners will have expended much sweat in attacking and countering each other, in a bout lasting two to three minutes! It is a test of stamina, agility and coordination of body and mind.

## HIKITATEGEIKO

In this stage the action is stepped up although the format of a controlled timed bout, with each partner successively acting as *tori* and *uke*, is identical to *kakarigeiko*. However, in *hikitategeiko*,

*uke* no longer takes up prescribed defensive postures, but resists *tori* using natural body movement and evasion. This gives *tori* (the defender) the opportunity to combine techniques in response to the resistance and movement of *uke* (the attacker) as the situation demands, learning to make judgements about timing and finding an opening in *uke*'s defences.

## RANDORIGEIKO

*Randorigeiko* is the ultimate progression. Here the roles of *tori* and *uke* are interchangeable, each partner freely applying techniques in response to the movements of the other.

In *toshu randorigeiko* each player will try to manoeuvre the other into a position where their balance is broken and they can be thrown or controlled with a lock. Grappling with each other is discouraged by the application of *atemi* counter-techniques, ensuring that a distance apart or proper defensive body spacing is maintained.

*Tanto randorigeiko*, requires one player to assume the primary role of attacker for half the timed period, against a defender using aikido technique. However, the attacker may also resist technique applied by the defender by using any one of five prescribed *atemi* techniques in their free-style form.

These training contests are rigorously controlled to maintain safety, but they are real tests of stamina, determination and the creative use of skills. They could be compared to a boxing sparring bout in the intensity of mental and physical effort required.

## SHIAI

*Shiai* is the practice of *tanto* or *toshu randorigeiko*, within a framework of established rules. It is therefore the practice of *randori* for competition. This form of training introduces the student to the rules of *shiai*, or contest, and the rhythm and manner of its play.

Just as it would be impossible to learn to play tennis without ever having played a practice match, so it is with *Tomiki Aikido*. While at some point in their training all *Tomiki Aikido* students will be introduced to the elements of randori match play, and learn how to operate within its rules, they are no more or less likely to take part in any formal competition or championship than the average tennis club player. Training for national and international championships is pursued by a minority of *Tomiki Aikido* students, as is the case with any other modern martial art.

However, *shiai*, is often demonstrated at annual club and inter-club events and public displays to illustrate the outcomes of *randori* training. A demonstration of *shiai*, although contested for a win, is obviously not entered into with the same spirit as a championship event. It is played to demonstrate good *tais-abaki* and fast, light, aikido techniques.

## THE CHARACTER OF A TOMIKI AIKIDO DOJO

In terms of philosophy and technique, *Tomiki Aikido*'s sport orientation might lead one to assume that the character of a *Tomiki Aikido dojo* reflected this. Undoubtedly much of the *randori* training is more physical than other styles of aikido, in that techniques are attempted on partners who are actively trying to counter and resist. This is not the practice in any other major style of aikido which stems from the teaching of Morihei Ueshiba, and undoubtedly requires high levels of fitness to be competently performed. However, competition is only one element of an extensive curriculum, which is as much centred on *kata* and the understanding of the fundamentals of aikido as any other style.

The promotion of health and well-being through an activity that is pleasurable, absorbing and perhaps even challenging, is understood universally as the *raison d'etre* for participation in sports. The keynote of the growth of mass participation in sport is that it clarifies these uncomplicated aims, and makes both the nature of the activity, and the technical proficiency required, accessible to the average citizen. This is what *Tomiki Aikido* sets out to do; to mediate the spiritual message of Morihei Ueshiba's aikido, through the methodologies of sport and the applied science of physical education.

This emphasis is reflected in the spirit of a *Tomiki Aikido dojo*, which although insisting on good discipline and the virtues of *reigi-saho*, or etiquette, keeps its rituals simple and easily understood. *Ki* is also a concept that is de-mystified; recognized as a physical process which is a conjunction of the fine-tuning of mind and body, spirit and technique, not an esoteric force that can be summoned or siphoned from the cosmos. This is plain, down to earth, sceptical aikido, which only believes what can be demonstrated effectively and taught accessibly.

Much of this character is inherited from its birthplace in the Physical Education faculty of Tokyo's Waseda University. This has given *Tomiki Aikido* a more open democratic spirit, both in the manner in which teachers communicate with students and in the conduct of *Tomiki Aikido* organisations around the world. Although within Japan itself the nature of *Tomiki Aikido dojo* regimes might be more severe than in the West, they are far more open and animated than many aikido schools.

The traditional black or dark blue *hakama*, or culottes style trousers, worn in most styles of aikido by dan grades, is rarely seen in the *Tomiki Aikido dojo*. Most training is conducted in the traditional *keigogi* (white judo-style jacket and trousers) which is more appropriate to the fast evasive action and counter moves of *randori* training, where a *hakama* would be an unnecessary impediment. *Hakama* are worn by dan grades for special exhibition events and sometimes for the performance of *embu* in competitive events. This is not, however, the requirement of any rule and is regarded as a matter of personal preference.

Women have had an important part in the development of *Tomiki Aikido*, particularly within both the UK and the USA. This is exemplified by Britain's Dr Ah Loi Lee, who has the distinction of being one of the few 7th Dan, women or men, in the aikido world. Competition for women has developed alongside that of the men and though the events, particularly *tanto randori*, attract less support than the men's events, they achieve high standards. In 1997, Chandra Kaur and Vanda Fairchild of the British *Aikido* Association, had the distinction of winning 1st and 3rd places respectively for women's *tanto randori shiai* at the 3rd International *Tomiki Aikido* Tournament, in Imabari, Japan.

The martial arts *dojo*, can still be a very daunting place for a woman, when first entered, but she can be sure that *Tomiki Aikido*, in line with its educational philosophy, sees issues of openness and equality as important.

This open democratic spirit can also be witnessed in the participation of ethnic minorities within its ranks and their representation in national squads, which have truly reflected the multi-ethnic cultures of modern Europe and America.

The major strength of *Tomiki Aikido* is still centred in Japan, within the Japanese universities, with Waseda University and the *Shodokan Dojo* in Osaka being major centres for research and experimentation in the style. Research and development is a major characteristic of *Tomiki Aikido*, as modifying and adapting technique to meet the needs of dynamic competition becomes a strong force for change. This keeps the style young and fresh, and the debate between senior teachers lively!

Tetsuro Nariyama *Sensei*, 8th Dan, heads the *Shodokan Dojo* in Osaka, which has become a leading centre in the technical development of the style and a mecca for foreign *aikidoka*. Many of the emerging new leaders of the style have been taught by him both in Japan and on his extensive tours to Australia, America and Europe. His partner in this enterprise has been

Fumiaki Shishida *Sensei*, 7th Dan, also a Professor at Waseda University in the tradition of the founder, Kenji Tomiki *Sensei*. Nariyama and Shishida jointly head the *Shihan* Division of the Japan Aikido Association, responsible for the technical development of the style and the maintenance of standards. The current head of the style is Tomiki *Sensei*'s widow, Fusae Tomiki, ably backed by the Chairman of the JAA, Riki Kogure *Sensei*, 8th Dan. *Tomiki Aikido* is associated worldwide through the 'Tomiki Aikido International Network', (TAIN) which brings together national associations to debate and plan international events and to promote the dissemination of research from Japan. Naturally, Japan represents the dominant force in *Tomiki Aikido*, but the JAA claims no international authority. Each national association is self-governing and receives no directives from Japan. It is the technical example set by the JAA, together with the warm humanity of the style's senior Japanese instructors, which maintain their leading position in international *Tomiki Aikido* affairs.

Spiritual gains, as we have seen, are implicit rather than explicit in the process of learning *Tomiki Aikido* and are very much the private preserve of the individual. The kind of austere discipline on the long road to spiritual enlightenment undertaken by Ueshiba is not easily replicated by ordinary people, who are concerned with families, health and busy jobs. *Tomiki Aikido* says to its adherents, we cannot guarantee to make you into another Ueshiba *Sensei*, but we can give you an efficient, practical and dynamic style of training that produces high level aikido skills. For many *Tomiki Aikido* students this is more than enough.

# 8

# THE KI-POWERED WAY: KOICHI TOHEI AND SHIN SHIN TOITSU AIKIDO

Of all the defections from the mainstream led by prominent students of Morihei Ueshiba, perhaps the most surprising was that of Koichi Tohei, 10th Dan, a close personal student of Morihei Ueshiba and one-time Chief of the Instruction Department at the *Aikikai Hombu Dojo*.

Koichi Tohei began his practice of aikido in 1939, after illness had curtailed his judo career and at a time when he was looking for spiritual as well as physical health and direction. His training was interrupted by World War II, but he returned to intensive training soon after the war, making a rapid rise through the aikido hierarchy. He was a considerable force in the post-war development of aikido and was responsible, almost single-handedly, for the birth of aikido in Hawaii and all over mainland U.S.A.

Tohei *Sensei* enjoyed the confidence of Morihei Ueshiba and was awarded his 8th Dan by O *Sensei* in 1952. Tohei went to Hawaii in 1953 and stayed for three years and, as a result, is one of the few Japanese masters of aikido able to speak fluent English. This ability, coupled with his charm and charisma have served him well in popularising aikido worldwide.

Tohei *Sensei* served as a Technical Director of the Instruction Branch of the *Aikikai* and was officially awarded his 10th Dan in

1970. Tohei *Sensei* had come to believe that however important it might be for aikido to be an effective means of self-defence, Morihei Ueshiba had shown that aikido was a true *budo* and primarily a way of spiritual improvement. *Ki* is the essential component of this Way and over the course of the next ten years Tohei watched with increasing disquiet what he saw as a decline in demonstrating and emphasising the importance of *ki* in the teaching of aikido. While Ueshiba *Sensei* was alive this stress on *ki* was maintained, but with his death it seemed to Tohei that many of his fellow instructors began to view the whole question of *ki* development as irrelevant.

Tohei began to develop a powerful critique of the methods and ideology of the *Aikikai*, from his vantage point as the Chief Instructor of the *Hombu Dojo*. Tohei felt that it was comparatively easy to teach people the techniques of aikido, because they represent the outside of the process. The real learning lay in the invisible processes of mind leading mind. This learning could not just be left to chance but must be taught, nurtured and developed just like any other kind of learning. Tohei *Sensei* maintained that, 'to throw others is of little use for ordinary people in their daily lives. The purpose of aikido training is to control mind and body and obtain the power of unification of mind and body'.

The deeply felt differences about the future direction of aikido between Kisshomaru Ueshiba, other senior teachers at the Hombu on one side and Tohei and his supporters on the other, developed into a hostile feud. Tohei felt that his new ideas for teaching aikido would be stifled and his students refused ranking recognition if he remained loyal to the *Aikikai*. Accordingly, he felt bound to separate from the *Aikikai* on 1 May 1974.

Following this formal separation, heralded by sending a letter to hundreds of *dojo* heads in Japan and throughout the world explaining his reasons, he set up his own organisation.

The Aikikai reacted with great hostility to Tohei *Sensei*'s position and circulated many *dojo*, requiring them to have no further contact with him, and he no longer enjoyed the confidence of the *Doshu* Kisshomaru Ueshiba and the *Aikikai Hombu*. While many of his closest supporters and students throughout the world decided to leave with him, Tohei *Sensei* saw many others take his picture down from their *dojo* walls and sever relations. It was a bitter and unpleasant time which, due to Tohei's great prominence and closeness to Ueshiba *Sensei*, opened a rancorous schism in aikido that is still not fully healed.

Tohei *Sensei* founded a style which he called, *Shin Shin Toitsu Aikido* (Aikido with Mind and Body Coordinated), which is represented through the *Shin Shin Toitsu Aikidokai* and the *Ki No Kenkyukai* (Ki Research Society), both formed in May 1974.

Tohei's school emphasises the importance of *ki* and is distinguished by a series of *ki* development exercises and breathing practices in combination with soft, flowing aikido technique. Tohei *Sensei* continues to teach and travels extensively throughout the world. He has recently opened a large *dojo* complex, retreat and *ki* training centre in Tochigi Prefecture.

## SHIN SHIN TOITSU AIKIDO: THE PHILOSOPHY OF PRACTICE

Tohei Sensei's acrimonious departure from the mainstream may have wounded the aikido family temporarily, leading many old friends to fall out. Yet it enabled him to embark on the creation of an aikido that has come to emphasise the development of *ki*, as a tangible experience open to all.

Tohei believed it was possible to shortcut the long ascetic training and profound metaphysical studies he and his teacher Ueshiba had undergone, and to develop a practice which would extend one's human fund of *ki*. Nothing would be left to the chance, instead *ki* could be realised by, 'unifying the mind and the body'. Why? To bring health, happiness and success and to fulfil the human potential. His message is clear and simple; *ki* can be extended and developed by teaching people how to coordinate their minds and their bodies. Aikido is the vehicle by which this can be done. But the practice must make this explicit and teach a progressive, developmental practice that combines specific exercises and aikido technique to develop *ki*.

## WHAT IS KI?

Within Tohei *Sensei*'s system *ki* is seen as the 'undivisable substance of the universe', the 'nearly nothing' from which man emerges. *Ki*, Tohei believes, can be equated with what Christians call 'God' and Buddhists call 'Buddha', the creating force which forms and animates life.

We experience this life through the interaction of opposing forces in the relative world, which is seen as the tension between the two opposing forces of *yin* (negative) and *yang*, (positive). *Ki*, generated by the brain and imagined as electromagnetic energy, adopts this positive or negative character and determines our health and well-being. Negativity drains our store of *ki* and leads to a downward spiral of indifferent health and depression. For Tohei 'no borders exist between mind and body in this process'; both must be nurtured to extend *ki*. Strengthening one without the other leaves the mind and body uncoordinated and out of balance.

If, then, you wish to be happy and content you must think and act positively, developing your stamina, physical power and the calm relaxed mind that will increase your *ki* and animate your life. Tohei describes aikido as a new and modern process for *ki*-development, acting as a 'bridge between psychology, which concerns itself exclusively with the mind, and physical education, which deals only with the body.'

Aikido can only have one true purpose; to develop and extend our *ki*, by teaching us simply and effectively to coordinate our mind and body.

## WHAT IS KI DEVELOPMENT?

*Shin Shin Toitsu Aikido*'s articulation of *ki* development is through the observance of Tohei *Sensei*'s four principles of mind and body coordination, around which all its practice is centred. They are the four descriptors of a single state, the unified mind and body. If one principle is maintained then the other three will automatically be satisfied. Conversely, if one principle is missing then the other three principles are also lost.

As descriptors of the same condition they are best described by practical demonstration of the positive effects they have on one's stability, command of movement and sense of inner calm. This forms the basis for *ki* testing, a central component of Tohei's system that distinguishes *Shin Shin Toitsu* or more colloquially *Ki Aikido* from all the other aikido styles.

The *Shin Shin Toitsu* practitioner learns to combine the practice of aikido technique with a progressive process of *ki* exercises. These exercises enhance and develop the practitioner's awareness of *ki* and how to extend and use it, not only within the *dojo*, which is only a place to learn and experiment, but in our everyday lives.

*Ki* extension can be taught independently of aikido if so wished and Tohei, always a canny publicist, has gained fame from instructing professional golfers, baseball stars and *sumo* wrestlers in using his methods to enhance their performance. Tohei also emphasises the importance of *ki* development for the world of business and has conducted seminars and lectures advocating the application of his principles to guarantee business success.

The ability to summon and extend *ki* gives us the ability to command a positive energy that can be transferred into every area of our lives. This is unequivocally a philosophy primarily concerned with health, both physical and mental. To demonstrate the power of *ki* in an actual healing context, Tohei *Sensei* has devised a system of massage called *kiatsu*, which is taught as an integral part of its curriculum. Although *budo* teachers have traditionally combined the roles of martial artist and healer, setting bones, providing herbal remedies and massage, within the modern *budo* systems formal teaching of healing skills is virtually defunct. *Shin Shin Toitsu Aikido* is the only major style of aikido which has developed a complementary healing system.

Tohei *Sensei* tells us that the ability to summon and command *ki* is not only possible, but is tangible and can be proved through demonstration. All that is required of us, is that we learn to maintain his 'Four Basic Principles'.

## THE FOUR BASIC PRINCIPLES

These principles are:

- Keep 'one point'.
- Relax completely.
- Keep weight underside.
- Extend *ki*.

### KEEP 'ONE POINT'

Keeping the 'one point' is a precept for the mind, not for the body, but as the mind moves the body, it can be demonstrated physically. The ability to understand and use this principle will enable the practitioner to develop a state of concentrated calm, the immovable mind within the immovable body.

The 'one point' is visualized as being at the centre of the universe which is infinite in dimension. That centre can be imagined as being seated within us in the *seika-no-itten*, or the 'one point in the lower abdomen', visualized by our mind 10cm below the navel. Even if we sit in a crossed-legged *zazen* position locating our strength low within our abdomen, keeping the spine stretched and our nose and navel in line to 'sit like a rock' as the Zen masters demand, we can still easily be pushed over. True strength relies on calming the mind, by imagining the centre of the universe as a diminishing sphere, infinitely halving itself until it resides at the 'one point' below your navel. This process of meditational visualization will enable you to concentrate the mind, in order to free and relax the body. Now, if you maintain that concentration and you are seated in *zazen*, you will remain calm and immovable when pushed. Relax the mind and let it wander, and your stability will be lost.

## RELAX COMPLETELY

Relaxation has become a modern fixation, much spoken of by health practitioners as an important weapon in our fight against stress and mental ill health. It is rarely effectively practised. It is Tohei's view that people conceive of this as a 'pleasant but weak state' causing us to 'revert to tension' whenever we are put under pressure. Physical exercises cannot give us the complete relaxation we need. To relax completely we must concentrate on the 'one point'

This will produce a relaxed but truly strong state, that can once again be demonstrated. The practitioner 'keeps the one point', stands with arms loose at his sides and elbows naturally bent, then shakes his hands vigorously to release all the tension in the body. His partner takes hold of his wrist and pushes up towards his shoulder. Even with a good sense of balance, his arm will be moved and he will become unstable. The *ki aikidoka* then repeats the exercise, this time shaking his hands vigorously for 20 to 30 seconds, ensuring the whole body shakes around the 'one point'. When his partner again attempts to push up his wrist, he is found to be immovable.

If we dispel all the tension in our bodies we will be able to relax completely and the mind will be calm at the 'one point' in the lower abdomen.

## KEEP WEIGHT UNDERSIDE

Naturally the weight of all objects is found at its lowest point, its underside. Human beings are no less subject to this natural state but the mind can interfere with this process. The un-calm state will cause tension, bringing weight to our upper bodies and consequent *dis*balance. Calm the mind, keep the 'one point' and relax completely and your weight will return to where it should be, on the underside.

To test this principle the *ki aikidoka* may extend his arm forwards at shoulder level. If he concentrates his mind and thinks that his weight is on the underside of his arm, then his partner will not be able to push it up from underneath. If he repeats this exercise, now focusing his mind on his upper arm, then it will be easily pushed up. Keeping weight underside is therefore the corollary of relaxing completely.

If we practise such exercises at home, or before facing the tensions and stresses of our working lives then we will stay calm and effective.

## EXTEND KI

There is no strong *ki* or weak *ki*, there is only *ki* that is poorly extended or *ki* that is fully extended. This is the strong state. Extending our *ki* is a projection of the mind; a transmission of mental energy which has been nurtured by relaxing completely and keeping the 'one point' and weight underside.

This mental transmission can be demonstrated by the classic aikido *ki* test, described as the 'unbendable arm'. The practitioner once again projects his arm forwards at shoulder level, imagining that all his mental power, his *ki*, is flowing along through his arm and out through his finger tips, like water gushing out from a hose pipe. He puts no strength or tension in his arm but keeps the 'one point', relaxing completely. His partner takes a grip on the wrist and in the crook of the elbow and attempts to bend it back towards the shoulder. If the mental projection is maintained then the arm will not bend. When the experiment is repeated, this time flexing and tensing the muscles to resist one's partners actions, then, providing both of you are of equivalent strength, the arm will be easily bent. This is what is meant by extending *ki*.

It would be impossible to keep all these precepts constantly in mind, but because of their interchangeability, focusing the mind on one principle will naturally put the others in place. The Four Principles provide a methodology for gaining *fudoshin*, or the immovable mind; a state of crystal alertness embedded in the calm centre.

## HOW IS SHIN SHIN TOITSU AIKIDO TAUGHT?

*Shin Shin Toitsu Aikido* is often thought of as the softest of the aikido arts. A claim that Tohei would not deny as long as we realise that softness does not imply any lack of power or effectiveness. Indeed it would be *Ki Aikido*'s contention that the reverse is true, for lodged at the heart of their practice is the ability to extend *ki*. This ability transforms technique, stripping it to its essentials so that it relies on the minimum of physical manipulation and body movement to achieve its aim. The true strength gained by *ki* development enables the *Ki Aikido nage* to throw *uke* with a graceful, stylish minimalism that is outwardly the gentlest of all the major styles.

*Ki* tests are a non-aggressive and non-competitive way of testing the *aikidoka*'s *ki* extension and consequently his effectiveness in the performance of technique. A self-defence art practised

according to the principles of non-competition, where partners cooperate, finds true ability difficult to test. How can you judge whether *nage* really threw *uke*, or did *uke* cooperate and take the fall only because that is what he or she is expected to do? Whereas Tomiki *Sensei* answered the question of testing effectiveness through the use of *randori* and sporting contests, Tohei proposes the alternative of the *ki* test.

Training in *Shin Shin Toitsu Aikido* begins as one would expect in teaching the student to sit, bow and walk; good carriage being the essential prerequisite for developing a strong aikido posture. It proceeds with basic exercises and techniques that introduce the students to *ki* and how, by adopting various postures and movements of hips and limbs, it can be utilized. These exercises are always tests for 'strength, stability and balance', and therefore test the student's ability to 'keep the one point'. *Ki* tests provide instant feedback to the student, helping them to readjust their practice and not to become complacent about their skills. It is possible to concentrate long enough to pass tests in the *dojo*, but the important measure of success is whether you can maintain the 'one point' outside it.

Early in their training *Ki* aikido students are introduced to a further set of five principles that Tohei *Sensei* devised to inform their practice of aikido.

## THE FIVE PRINCIPLES OF KI AIKIDO

These are:

- Extend *ki*.
- Know your opponent's mind.
- Respect your opponent's *ki*.
- Put yourself in your opponent's place.
- Lead with confidence.

Extending *ki* requires the student to begin all actions with the mind and body coordinated. Your ability to extend *ki* will be tested by a partner testing you. This is done either by applying pressure from the hold itself, or from the direction of the attack. If your posture holds up and you meet the test, then you must progress to absorbing the next element into your practice.

### KNOW YOUR OPPONENT'S MIND

You must know how your opponent is attacking you, the speed and pace of his intentions and the strength of his grip. If he attacks with too much strength you may be able to throw him easily through efficiency of technique, but if on the other hand your opponent has his mind and body coordinated then you must use all the Five Principles. To begin to be able to measure and know your opponent's power, you must test him, again from the hold or the position of the attack. If your opponent's *ki* is strong and extended, you will find you cannot directly oppose him and you must seek to apply the third principle.

### RESPECT YOUR OPPONENT'S KI

To respect your opponent's *ki* is the ability to realise when it is senseless to resist or oppose a hold or attack. Where you have tested your opponent and found you cannot escape the hold, then you know you must use those parts of your body where he has no control, to counter the attack. These three principles relate to your:

- Control of your mind.
- Perception of your opponent's strength and capabilities, the application of these principles in movement.

All of these principles are continually measured against *ki* tests during practice.

## PUT YOURSELF IN YOUR OPPONENT'S PLACE

This means the skilful execution of technique so that your actions do not collide with your opponent or resist him directly. By the employment of *irimi* (entering) or *tenkan* (turning) you will be able to manoeuvre into a position where you are both facing the same direction, and you are able to lead him into the technique. This, of course, is the basis for all aikido technique and will take some years to learn before reaching *shodan*, or black belt, proficiency.

### LEAD WITH CONFIDENCE

Having absorbed all the first four principles and found that you can meet the *ki* tests at all the stages, you can now proceed to execute the immobilization or throw with your mind and body coordinated. Now, whether your opponent resists with all his physical strength or by the power of his own *ki*, you will be able to throw him or hold him down by employing the Five Principles.

## HOW THE KI AIKIDO CURRICULUM IS ORGANISED

*Ki Aikido* is organised into different levels. At the first level, students are taught the basics of posture, movement of the arms and hips and vitally of course, *ukemi* or falling safely. Simple basic techniques are introduced at this stage on which the student can start to base an understanding of the Five *Ki Aikido* Principles.

Progressing through six levels the student will be introduced to entering, turning, and attacks from different directions with the variety of holds and strikes common to all aikido. Finally the student will arrive through long training at a point where he or she can deal with attacks made with weapons or by multiple assailants.

Weapons are taught within the system although Tohei felt he received very little formal training from Ueshiba *Sensei* in the use of the *bokken* (sword). Through observation and his own experimentation, he developed his own principles for the use of the sword with mind and body unified. Great importance is placed on keeping the triangular stance and pointing the tip of the sword towards the opponent with *ki* extended.

All the usual aikido wooden training weapons are included in advanced practice, the *tanto* (knife), *bokken* (sword) and *jo* (staff). Whenever they are used, lightness of grasp is emphasized because tension, in the hands or body, prevent one from keeping the mind and body coordinated. The student must be able to feel the weapon as an extension of his own body and project *ki* through towards the opponent. Two sets of principles guide practice with sword and *jo*. These are:

For the *bokken*:

- Hold the *bokken* lightly.
- Keep the tip of the *bokken* unwavering.
- Make use of the *bokken*'s weight.
- Extend *ki* and concentrate on the 'one point'.
- Cut first with the mind.

For the *jo*:

- Hold the *jo* lightly.
- Control the *jo* with the rear hand.
- Manipulate the *jo* freely.
- Keep one hand on the *jo* whenever changing its position.
- The line traced by the *jo* is never broken.

Although *Shin Shin Toitsu Aikido* is a style that has resisted competitive aikido in the form of *shiai*, or all-out contests for mastery, it has accepted a form of competition that shares all the elements of *Tomiki Aikido*'s *kata embu* events. There is a trend detected running through all the major styles. This form of competition is called *Taigi* within *Shin Shin Toitsu Aikido*.

# TAIGI COMPETITION

Every year, Ki Society students come to Tokyo from all over Japan to take part in the *Taigi* Competition. In a sense it is a logical extension of the concept of *ki* testing. It provides the opportunity to test one's *ki*, with the added pressures of time constraint and performance in front of a friendly but critical audience. Sets of partners compete by performing the same sets of prescribed aikido techniques, which are then judged by three criteria;

- Quality of technique.
- Degree of mind and body coordination (*fudoshin*).
- Rhythm of the performance.

Marks are determined by a panel of judges and medals are awarded to the winning contestants. It is also the custom, providing the appropriate experience is evident, to promote the *nage* of the winning partnership by one dan grade, while silver and bronze finalists receive certificates of recognition and medals.

## HOW TAIGI IS CONTESTED

The partners, acting as *nage* and *uke*, must perform a set of six or more prescribed throws in the correct sequence within a given number of seconds, plus or minus two. Twelve or more throws may be achieved in under a minute, using as much space as possible and with effortless pace and precision. There must be no sense of panic and hurry. *Nage* will be watched for stability, mind and body unification and the degree of *ki* extension when executing the throws. Rhythm is judged by looking at the fluidity of technique, the coordination between *nage* and *uke*, the grace of movement and the presence of the performers.

All contestants compete against *aikidoka* of their own age range and rank, the different groups performing different *Taigi* sets appropriate to their age and their experience. Higher ranks will perform *Taigi* that use weapons and require sophisticated and developed skills to perform.

*Taigi* provides an incentive for the *ki aikidoka* to focus on during his or her training in order to hone and polish their performance for a special test. On the contest area, nervous and in front of your peers, there is an opportunity to measure whether you can truly keep 'one point'. Of course it also helps the Ki Society instructors to watch and measure their own standards across the *dojo* and inspire their students to greater efforts. Not least, it is also an important social occasion, cementing and extending friendships and bringing the Ki Society together as one.

*Taigi* competitions of this kind, although not yet of similar size and occasion, are staged by national associations in other parts of the world, and will doubtless grow with the spread of *Shin Shin Toitsu Aikido*.

## THE CHARACTER OF A SHIN SHIN TOITSU AIKIDO DOJO

The character of a *Shin Shin Toitsu Aikido dojo* differs little in terms of etiquette and formal procedures from that of the *Aikikai*, or the *Yoshinkan*, save for pictures of Tohei *Sensei* and calligraphy that reflects *Ki Aikido* tenets. *Ki Aikido* practitioners wear the familiar training suit, with white belts worn until they are exchanged for black when reaching *shodan*, or 1st dan. *Hakama*, in common with the *Aikikai*, are worn in practice as they help emphasise good posture. It is considered that by hiding the feet, the *hakama* assists in maintaining calm dignity.

Where differences occur they relate to those parts of the lesson where the *Ki Aikido* student is being taught how to develop understanding of *ki*. As we have seen, *ki*-exercises and their component *ki*-tests will form an important part of the lesson and would be an unfamiliar practice for *aikidoka* from other styles.

Breathing is the important element in *ki*-development. Breathing in and out through the whole body is considered necessary to keep up the exchange of *ki* through the system. It is not surprising then, that more formal attention to breathing is given than in aikido's other systems. *Ki*-breathing is an exercise intended to produce a more natural, and deeper process of controlled breathing, which will eventually carry over in some measure to our everyday lives.

Students performing *ki*-breathing exercises sit in *seiza* with backs straight and hips settled. The student exhales through the mouth making a barely audible 'hah' sound, and continues to breath out for as long as the sound can be maintained. Once a limit is reached, the student gently leans forward ten degrees, and exhales the small amount of air that remains. The object is to empty the entire lung capacity, which is estimated to take about twenty five seconds. Few of us ever breath out for this long and it takes time and practice to perfect.

When the student is satisfied that all air has been expelled from the lungs and still with the upper body inclined, the mouth is closed and air is inhaled slowly through the nose, which Tohei describes as 'as if smelling a flower'; again with a necessary but barely audible sound, in order to monitor your capacity. Students are asked to imagine that the breath is filling their bodies from the feet up. This visualisation avoids self-conscious focus on the stomach and lungs, which may limit one's inhalation rather than prolong it. When the student feels that full lung capacity has been reached, the body is returned to upright and a further breath taken in. Once complete, the cycle is repeated. This is, of course, an exercise for the home as much as the *dojo* and one's aim should be to sustain a comfortable session for thirty to sixty minutes.

This exercise will also be supported with *ki*-meditation, where the student is asked to sit quietly in *seiza* with the eyes closed and the mind focused on the 'one point'. Posture is periodically tested for stability to check continued focus on the 'one point'.

The performance of technique is also qualitatively different, as there is a stylised minimalism in its execution, which avoids powerful balance breaking or dramatic use of *atemi*. Any sense of aggressiveness is dispelled from technique by the gentle leading of *uke* through the required pattern of movement. *Ki Aikido* is not orientated towards practical self-defence as would be true of other styles. The *ki* student is more concerned with the protection of health and the power that aikido generates for that purpose, rather than its effectiveness in dealing with muggers.

The gentle quality of technique has an appeal for those similarly attracted to tai chi or yoga, as *Ki Aikido* is a system directed towards the preservation of health and vitality. In addition it has many solo development exercises that can be practised at home. *Ki Aikido*'s student profile is similar to other styles in the proportions of young to old and women to men, but it has obvious appeal to those put off by the more forceful practice of other styles.

Uniquely, Tohei's system is also a route to learning how to use *ki* to heal others with *kiatsu* therapy. *Kiatsu*, literally *ki* pressure, unlike *shiatsu* or acupuncture makes no use of meridians or specific points on the body. Neither is the body manipulated or given deep finger pressure massage. Instead light pressure is applied perpendicularly to the muscle through the fingertips. The therapist fixes his or her mind on the 'one point' and extends *ki*, transmitting it into the patient's body. This has far more in common with *reiki*, where *ki* is similarly exchanged but, in this case, through the palms of the hands. *Ki* is seen as

flowing throughout the body and across the total surface of the skin, not restricted to flowing through prescribed channels. *Ki* infuses our whole selves. Therefore, there are no specific points of treatment. It is a slow healing that helps us to build up and re-energise our system through a transfer of *ki*-energy.

This singular focus on the transforming power of *ki*, has led the *Ki No Kenkyukai* (Ki Research Society), to establish one of the most impressive institutions in the martial arts world. The *Ki no Sato*, or 'Homeland of Ki' is named for its location on the property where Tohei *Sensei* spent his youth. It is a massive complex covering some 30,000 square metres of land, comprising a Ki Meditation Hall (*Tenshin Gosho*), a *Misogi* Bathing Hall for purification exercises, a *Kiatsu* Therapy Training Hall and the Main *Dojo* itself. The Main *Dojo* is an impressive 2,000 square metre space with a ceiling 14 metres high. Equipped with 520 *tatami* mats it is the largest *dojo* in Japan.

The site also includes dormitory facilities, extensive gardens surrounding the Tohei family's ancestral home, a 300 year old magistrate's house, and finally the Museum of Ki. This institution conducts research into establishing a scientific basis for the existence of *ki* and mounts exhibitions of the historical, cultural and clinical evidence collected. The Museum of Ki is visited by significant numbers, not only for its exhibitions, but for the peace and tranquillity of the site. *Ki no Sato* also offers long term residential training courses for *Ki Aikido* instructors and *kiatsu* therapists, and a variety of shorter programmes for those wishing to study some aspect of Tohei *Sensei*'s system.

*Shin Shin Toitsu Aikido* has built a strong following throughout the world and is represented not only in Japan, but in the UK and other parts of Europe, the USA, and the Pacific Rim, including Australia, New Zealand, Singapore and Indonesia. *Ki Aikido*'s primary concern with health and the conquest of stress, makes it an ideal aikido for those seeking a unified defence for living.

# WHAT KIND OF AIKIDO?

## HOW DO I CHOOSE A CLASS?

Any potential student of aikido ought first to consider what it is about this martial art that attracts their interest, before looking for a teacher and a *dojo*. If time is taken to reflect on some basic questions, then it will be possible to create a checklist of needs and preferences against which you can match what is on offer. Aikido is not a product that comes in standardised packages, and each *dojo* and teacher will differ in the manner and direction of their practice. Some of these differences will relate clearly to the character and skill of the teacher, the interaction of the students and the 'spirit' or atmosphere in the *dojo*, while others will be about the differences between schools or styles of aikido.

## WHAT AM I LOOKING FOR?

Experience shows that the majority of students who come through the doors of a *dojo* for the first time give one or more of the following reasons for wishing to study aikido. These are:

- To get fit.
- To learn to defend themselves.
- To have fun (social interaction).
- To develop themselves mentally or spiritually.

130     Most *aikidoka* would confess to having begun with the same
shopping list, all bound up with the exotic expectations that go
with learning a martial art. Therefore we can assume there is
also a belief that an 'Eastern' approach to finding a good way of
living, will bring more solid benefits than boxercise, or aerobics. This is the intangible element of the quest; the question
that cannot quite be framed by reason and is only answered in
the doing. Whatever brought the potential student to the *dojo* in
the first place, it is unlikely that the same motives will keep
them returning for twenty years or more. The rewards of aikido
come only with time and patient commitment. When questions
begin to be answered before you have thought of them, then
you will know why you stayed.

However, before we assume the confidence to pass through
that *dojo* door, let us put some flesh on some basic questions
that we may have in mind.

## WILL AIKIDO KEEP ME FIT?

Aikido will keep you fit, but you may have to examine what
you mean by fitness. Aikido will not provide the intense, sustained work out provided by aerobics. It will have periods of
intense activity that are physically demanding, but there will
also be many periods of quiet instruction where you can
recover. A good *sensei* will find ways to integrate you into
meaningful practice whatever your starting point and encourage you to find a level of fitness where you are challenged, but
can still perform comfortably.

Aikido takes a holistic approach to fitness, seeing the cultivation of a calm, centred mind as the development of a fit and
supple body. The physical benefits of aikido come through
the ability to meet stress and conflict in daily life with the same
confidence as in the *dojo*, finding a flexible non-confrontational
way through life. This said, some *dojo* will require more stamina

and physical effort than others and often this will tend to reflect the style of the aikido practised.

Obviously a sports orientated style such as *Tomiki Aikido* requires levels of fitness from its championship competitors comparable to Olympic Judo players. But that would be the tip of a pyramid with a very broad base and certainly not expected of the average club member. Alternatively, at the other end of the spectrum, *Shin Shin Toitsu Aikido* offers a combination of 'soft' flowing technique and exercises designed to encourage relaxation, the control of breath and the summoning of *ki*. Exercise in the *dojo* will be vigorous, but it will not require the same character of fitness as the *Tomiki Aikido* free-style contest bout.

The style of aikido does have a bearing on fitness, but is more conditioned by the level you wish to perform at. All styles require fitness for peak performance. The best way for you to find out what is required, is to visit more than one *dojo* and watch the practice. You will know what you feel comfortable with.

## WILL AIKIDO TEACH ME HOW TO DEFEND MYSELF?

Aikido is a self-defence system of devastating effectiveness, but it requires subtlety, sensitivity and technical precision to perform well. It is not a quick route to basic self-defence skills and will not provide you with a course where you can learn a few things to protect yourself. It may not at first fill you with any confidence at all, as the techniques will be difficult to perform until the mind and body learn to work together. However, long-term training aims to give you the ability to act instinctively in your own defence, with an alert mind and a calm centre. Aikido approaches the question of personal protection from the premise that the best form of self-defence is one you do not have to use. It is in the avoidance of conflict that ultimate safety is ensured.

Again, the style and the character of the *sensei* will determine the emphasis put on the realistic rehearsal of self-defence skills. *Yoshinkan Aikido* attaches great importance to a sturdy posture that can stand a blow and the delivery of robust *atemi*, before applying aikido techniques. On the other hand, mainstream aikido of the *Aikikai* Foundation, would place more emphasis on evasive and circular patterns of manoeuvre.

While all styles can help you to develop awareness and basic self-defence confidence, the degree of importance you attach to this will have to be another question to ask yourself. If it is only self-defence skills that you wish to learn, then aikido will not be the easiest Way to find them. If you wish to learn to defend your whole life then it has much to offer.

## WILL I HAVE FUN?

If aikido was joyless, then there would be little point in talking about *budo* as love or peace. Aikido aims to be a joyful activity, engaged in with seriousness and discipline, but full of physical verve and emotional intensity. It celebrates life through harmonious movement, which has to be shared with a partner to be understood. It is of essence sociable, as you need someone else to practise it with. There are no solo forms. To get on in aikido you have to be able to get on with people, confirming the physical trust you place in each other when practising potentially dangerous techniques. This helps to build some very solid friendships. A good *dojo* should be a gathering of friends, enthusiastically engaged in a common purpose.

Like all human activity, aikido will have its share of rogue or unpleasant characters, but the decency and respect for others required of the *aikidoka* keeps check on these traits during practice. No *sensei* of integrity will allow bullying or spiteful behaviour in the *dojo*.

Beyond the *dojo*, there is of course the social activity generated by the club after practice. Associations organise seminars and holiday courses, which can be international in character and involve home-stays and camps across the globe. All the bigger associations have these programmes and contacts, maintaining close relationships with senior teachers in Japan and worldwide. Membership of associations with this international character can allow you to walk through the doors of any *dojo* and find a welcome and an invitation to practise, provided the local forms are observed. If you want a wider circle, then aikido may help you find one.

## CAN I DEVELOP MYSELF MENTALLY AND SPIRITUALLY?

As we have seen in previous chapters, aikido is primarily concerned with development of *wa*, or harmony, and the cultivation of the body and mind in order to create a peaceful reconciliation with yourself, your surroundings and others. This requires mental discipline to reach and spiritual insight to secure. However, this is not a way of 'faith' and its spirituality is not founded in any need to believe in one religious truth. Aikido's spiritual path aims to deepen your understanding of self and place and enable you to act spontaneously in an open compassionate manner.

*Ki* is fundamental to this spiritual purpose, but the source of ideological difference between aikido allegiances lies in its interpretation. While some would see *ki* as the expression of tangible physical actions, others might view it as the ability to tap into a force that is both inside and outside the self. This attitude marks important differences in the practice of individual styles, which may not be immediately apparent when watching an aikido class for the first time. But the spiritual emphasis put on practice can often be read in how people train and the

respect shown to *dojo* etiquette and forms. While this is not the only criterion you should use, it is a useful indicator. The only sure way to locate yourself in the right place, is to ask the *sensei* his or her views and how they relate to the training in their *dojo*. Then see for yourself how they match.

## WHAT DO ALL DOJO HAVE IN COMMON?
### A 'SOFT' ART

In general aikido *dojo* are warm and friendly places that no beginner should fear. In choosing aikido rather than the higher profile boxing and kicking martial arts, you have already made a commitment to the defensive, and rejected the option of the offensive. This should help place where you stand on issues of conflict and its resolution, and is likely to indicate that others in the *dojo* will also share your values. Aikido is not a martial art that attracts the would be street-fighter. It is normally characterised as a 'soft' or 'internal' martial art alongside its older Chinese counterpart tai chi. 'Soft' martial arts have rejected aggressive and brutal solutions to conflict, and aim to develop our 'internal' senses to better command the energies of the body. You should expect all aikido *dojo* to reflect the ethical idealism of the Founder, in the open and generous spirit of the training and the shared care and concern for each other's progress in the art.

Open in spirit, must mean open to all. Aikido will never exclude anyone, irrespective of any race, religion or gender, who comes through the *dojo* door in the same open spirit and is willing to learn. Since the death of *O Sensei*, aikido has spread to every continent and is practised by peoples of every political and religious persuasion. The purpose of aikido is to explore *ki*, the universal spirit force that animates us all, not to find ways of dividing and excluding.

The qualities of the teacher are of paramount importance, as you will depend on the foundation they give you for your progress in the art. In your early aikido career, the bulk of learning and development in the art is likely to be the responsibility of one teacher. If you do not have confidence in the *sensei* you will not succeed. Human qualities of consideration, respect, enthusiasm, inspiration and friendliness we can all measure for ourselves and make our own judgements about. What is far more difficult is judging technical standards.

It is important to check the credentials of the *sensei* to see if he or she is supported and trained by a reputable aikido organisation, which has the authority to issue rank and ensure standards. In Japan, the UK, France and other countries, aikido organisations are registered with government sponsored control authorities or sports ministries, who police these standards. As a quality control assurance, it is best to enquire with the associations whose clubs are registered in your area.

Membership and registration of a recognised aikido association should also mean that your *sensei* has attended a coaching course and qualified as an instructor, which grade alone does not confer. Again, the recognised associations have active coaching programmes and require their coaches and instructors to carry public liability insurance and some knowledge of first-aid. These are the basic standards you should assure yourself of when considering a *dojo* to study in.

There are independent *dojo*, who may have teachers of a very high standard. Here, you need to know the reasons for that independence and the provenance or history of the teacher. Where did he or she learn aikido? Where was his or her rank awarded? By whom? Are they insured for public liability? If the *sensei* cannot or will not answer these questions satisfactorily, then it might be better to look around for another aikido *dojo*.

# BEGINNERS

Many clubs run special beginner classes where you will be among others in the same starting position. This can be a less daunting introduction than joining a regular class, where there will be *aikidoka* of all ranks and abilities. However, you should not be put off in these circumstances for you will find *aikidoka* eager to pass on what they know and consolidate their own learning in the process. This is an obligation expected of *sempai*, or seniors; that they must play an active part in the development and progress of the *dojo* and their fellow *aikidoka*.

You will at some stage be required to purchase the special training suit, *keikogi* or *dogi*, but in many *dojo* you may be able to purchase training suits at discounted prices. Before rushing out and buying something expensive and possibly inappropriate, check what you are expected to wear as a beginner with the club. Most clubs will allow you to train in a track suit or other loose fitting garments for a few sessions, before you are expected to make a commitment.

## GRADINGS

Although there are a few independent clubs that do not issue grades or rank, aikido has an organised ranking system, where your performance can be assessed from beginner stage, through general competence and on to mastery. It is an apprenticeship, with recognised stages of achievement marking your passage.

The system of ranking is common to modern Japanese *budo* and is known as the *kyu dan* system. In this system of ranking the apprenticeship level is signified by the *kyu* ranks, ranging in order from beginner level, which may start at 8th *kyu* or 6th *kyu*, and end at 1st *kyu*, within sight of the black belt. These grades are distinguished by the wearing of different coloured belts, which may differ according to association but usually start with white and progress through yellow, orange, green and blue to end at brown, the grade before black-belt.

Progress through the *kyu* ranks brings you eventually to *shodan*, or 1st dan, and the award of the much coveted and respected black belt, as well as the sanction to wear the *hakama*. Perhaps too well respected in the West, 1st dan merely signifies that the aikidoka has completed a three to five year training, depending on the intensity of practice. Beyond 1st dan, ranks are signified in ascending numerical order to 10th dan in some associations, or 9th dan in others.

The opportunity to grade is not merely a question of developing skill, as aikido requires a maturity of understanding. To encourage this, the minimum number of hours needed to be spent in practice before the next grading test are prescribed by the respective associations. Between dan rankings these time requirements are normally served out in numbers of years! This means that to have anything like senior rank at 5th dan or 6th dan level, you are likely to have been practising for over twenty years. Aikido has been a lifetime commitment for those who reach high rank, so beware young *sensei* who claim high grade, for many Japanese organisations with Western affiliates will not grade anyone below their thirties to ranks above 4th dan.

Grades should not become an obsession, they are a guide to and reward for your progress. They should never become a mark of superiority to be flaunted.

## MEMBERSHIP

The *dojo* you have selected will probably belong to an association which will collect an annual subscription. As a member you will be offered a programme of courses and events, the guarantee of standards of coaching and behaviour, the endorsement of your gradings and the issue of insurance. In many cases the association will be affiliated, or linked through an international body, to contacts in Japan, still the source of the highest quality instruction providing leadership and inspiration for the development of aikido. If some day you wish to visit and train in Japan, then membership of a group that has recognition and regular contact with a Japanese association will open doors to you. It is very likely that some of your own association's teachers will have received training at a senior level in Japan. It will also give you the opportunity to study with visiting Japanese masters.

## CHILDREN

Children are an important element of the life blood of many associations where junior membership can often equal that of the adult *aikidoka*. Aikido provides lessons about responsibility, care and concern for others, restraint and cooperation. By learning a way of defending yourself physically, *as a last resort*, you can have the confidence to walk away from fights and arguments. Fights escalate out of misunderstanding, mutual fear and lack of confidence. Aikido is about defeating the bully and not about providing the means to become one.

While the moral lessons of aikido are important, they are implicit in the practice of aikido and are not drummed in by long lectures and the chanting of rules. Aikido has to be fun for children and most junior classes will approach the teaching of aikido through a combination of games and techniques. The games will emphasize free movement of the body and the exercise of their limbs, or be concerned with developing social and cooperative skills necessary to aikido practice. Techniques will have been modified, with most associations avoiding techniques which rely on directly pressurising the joints of the body, limiting the junior curriculum to *atemi* or throwing moves. This is to avoid any possibility of damaging the vulnerable joints and bones of growing children.

As a sophisticated activity with much complex movement, the age at which one may start aikido will very much depend on the child's physical maturity, ability to concentrate and most of all, interest. There is no right or wrong age to start, but usually aikido clubs will have set some age limit and will not take children as young as they might in other martial arts. In the smaller clubs, you may find that children practise alongside the adults, or that the club has a special 'parents and children' session, providing the opportunity to practice aikido as a family.

### THE DISABLED

People with disabilities will know that their exclusion from activities can be more about the fears of the organisers than it is with danger or insurmountable difficulties. This is as true of aikido as any other activity. Disabled people are not as well represented as they should be, but there are *sensei* who are pioneering adapting techniques to the needs and capabilities of people with disabilities. Of course it depends on the type and degree of disability you have, your freedom of physical manoeuvre, levels of concentration and other factors. Constraints are compounded by aikido clubs practising in sports and community halls where access is limited and facilities for the disabled are poor.

If you are disabled and think you would be able to gain benefit from learning aikido, then your first course must be to find a teacher who is willing to find ways to make this possible. Often it is only the fact that the teacher has not been asked to teach someone in a wheelchair before, which has prevented them from developing approaches for people with this disadvantage, or any other. Technically aikido offers much scope for defending yourself while seated against a standing opponent, and could be adapted to many people with little or no use of their lower limbs.

The disabled person should not be put off. Contact a number of teachers and if possible visit their clubs to check access and suitability. Your actual appearance in the *dojo* may well be the best opportunity to convince the *sensei* that he or she can help you. One limiting factor may be the teacher's public liability insurance, but disabled sports associations may be able to assist with advice on this issue. The message is clear, it may take time and be more frustrating than it should be, but there are aikido *sensei* out there who will not turn you away when you arrive at their *dojo* door.

## HOW DOES AIKIDO TREAT WOMEN?

Women should have every expectation of complete equality of treatment in the world of aikido. This is an absolute human right and all *bona fide* aikido organisations forbid sexist, as indeed racist, behaviour. No one would expect the standards of any public organisation to be less, and their rule-books should give you an assurance that any complaints you might have are taken seriously.

As we all know, rules and regulations do not necessarily change personal attitudes and behaviour. The world of the martial arts has an image of *machismo*, of violent and aggressive behaviour that comes with an historic preserve of men; *fighting*. While this view may not represent a fair image of any modern martial *do* or Way, aikido was born from an Eastern culture where the social status of women has not been challenged to the same extent as in the West. This cultural inheritance is reflected in its hierarchical relationships and codes of behaviour, and are modelled on 'warrior' ethics which excluded women or relegated them to a minor role.

Despite this cultural history, aikido has been able to claim advantages in overcoming these attitudes and giving equal recognition to the skills and talents of women. The most

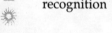

important of these advantages can be seen in the *dojo*, where size, weight and strength give no automatic advantage, but all the qualities in which women often excel – timing, flexibility and grace – count far more. There is absolutely no physical challenge in the practice of aikido that cannot be as easily accomplished by a woman as a man.

From the earliest days of aikido's history, women found a place in Ueshiba *Sensei's dojo*, although few took an equally active part. Although the social mores of those times gave women a lesser place, the very nature of aikido and its claim to be an inclusive, universally relevant *budo*, was an open door ready to be pushed. Today, there are many women teachers of high rank and status who teach throughout the world, where their seminars and courses receive as enthusiastic attendances as any senior male *sensei*.

As a woman, the fact that you will be able to perform as well and often better than your male partners, will give you the earned respect that is part of the fabric of the Eastern way of learning. What you may need to overcome are those doubts and fears that our society has conditioned you to feel in relation to men; such as a fear of being hurt physically, being touched, held down or thrown through the air. Ultimately, some courage is required, after all there would be no point to learning a martial discipline at all if it carried no element of physical challenge. This courage is required of all students. If you approach aikido on this basis you will be able to make your practice successful and be able to defend yourself as effectively as any man.

## WHAT STYLE OF AIKIDO SHOULD I PRACTISE?

We explained in this book that there is no 'one' aikido, but at least four major currents of interpretation that have formed into separate organisations with distinct practice and purposes. We have characterised these styles as the 'Traditional Way', the

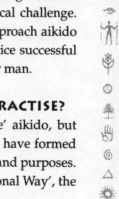

'Martial Way', the 'Sporting Way' and the '*Ki*-power Way'. Each of these styles appeals to different temperaments and serves different expectations, and all seek the same goals identified in Chapter 3. They are:

- The development of a healthy mind and body.
- The promotion of a decency and robustness of the spirit.
- The ability to live in harmony with your *self* and *all* around you.

Each of the styles will satisfy these purposes and more, for the real issue is not a matter of style but of the qualities and vision of the teacher. Look for a teacher that you can believe in, because that is the teacher who will believe in you.

Ueshiba *Sensei* believed that aikido should be practised to generate a positive understanding of *ki*, the force that drives the universe. The development and employment of *ki*, as the energy of positive action, can only be achieved if we learn to work in harmony with our world and not against it. Through the practice of aikido we learn, with our body and our mind, how to harmonise with a partner's movements, and how to avoid confrontation and redirect aggression. For those millions of us who seek the strength to lead a peaceful and constructive life, in a world where we are easily roused to anger, aikido is the means to gain that strength. This is a pathway for very modern warriors.

# GLOSSARY OF TERMS

*ai-hanmi* – mutual oblique position/stance take up by *nage* and *uke*.

*aiki* – harmony with *ki* (spirit), a principle applied in the execution of technique, similar in character to *ju* (see *ju*).

*Aiki Budo* – a name used to describe Morihei Ueshiba's aikido before World War II.

*aikidoka* – a committed practitioner of aikido.

*aikido kyogi* – sport aikido.

*aiki jujutsu* – unarmed self-defence systems utilizing the principle of *aiki*.

*atemi waza* – striking or impact applied against physiological weaknesses.

*awase* – to blend with the opponent's direction of movement and manner of attack.

*ayumi ashi* – corresponding to ordinary walking.

*bokken* – wooden sword, corresponding in shape to a *katana*, or samurai sword, used in aikido training.

*bu* – martial; pertaining to military combat.

*budo* – martial way.

*chushin* – central alignment.

*dan* – degree/ranking designation for black belt grades.

*do* – Way; a spiritual path to follow.

*dojo* – a place for teaching the Way; a training hall for teaching the martial Ways.

*Dojo Cho* – chief instructor of a *dojo*.

*Doshu* – 'Way Leader', used to describe the head of the *Aikikai* Foundation and the international movement of traditional aikido, Kisshomaru Ueshiba, the Founder's son and heir.

*embu* – a term used in *Tomiki Aikido* to describe the competitive performance of a sequence of aikido techniques (*kata*) by *tori* and *uke*, acting in partnership.

*go no sen* – to seize the initiative at the instant of attack and deliver a counter-attack.

*goshin* – self-defence.

*gyaku-hanmi* – reverse oblique position/stance taken up by *nage* and *uke*.

*gyo* – physical/spiritual exercise.

*hakama* – divided skirt-like trousers, worn as an item of traditional Japanese clothing by aikido dan (black belt) grades.

*hanmi hantachi waza* – aikido techniques applied when *nage* is seated and *uke* is standing.

*hara* – the 'belly', the centre of gravity within the body located in the lower abdomen and said to be the seat of *ki* and inner strength. Also described by the Buddhist term *tanden*.

*hidari* – left.

*hidarikamae* – left posture or stance.

*hiji-waza* – techniques that attack the elbow joints, and are applied against a stretched arm, or when the arm is entangled and bent.

*hombu dojo* – the headquarters *dojo* of a school of the martial arts or Way.

*ikkyo* – 'first teaching', the first *katame waza*, or pressure/joint locking technique. It is applied against the elbow.

*irimi* – an entering movement designed to bring *nage* in close to *uke*'s, body without meeting in a head-on clash.

*jo* – a wooden staff used in aikido training.

*joseki* – the upper side of the *dojo*.

*ju* – the principle of gentleness, suppleness, flexibility, pliability.

*jujutsu* – the art of applying the principle of flexibility; unarmed methods of self-defence.

*kaiten* – to enter and turn in combination.

*kake* – the application of the throw (*nage*), or joint-lock (*katame waza*), where *uke* is thrown to the ground and subdued.

*kamae* – a body position/posture taken up when facing an opponent.

*kamidana* – a small *Shinto* altar or shrine.

*kamiza* – upper seat.

*kata dori* – where *nage*'s shoulder is seized and held by *uke*.

*katame waza* – aikido techniques whereby *uke* is controlled by *nage* by means of anatomical pressure on the wrist, elbow and shoulder joints.

*katate dori* – where one of *nage*'s hand is seized and held by *uke*.

*keikogi* – or training suit.

*ken* – sword.

*kenjutsu* – *samurai* arts of swordsmanship intended for combat.

*ki* – the invisible force that animates the universe and gives power to life.

*kiatsu* – literally *ki* pressure, a form of finger pressure therapy used in *Shin Shin Toitsu Aikido*.

*kihon-dosa* – basic exercises that exemplify the patterns of aikido form, movement and posture in *Yoshinkan Aikido*.

*kihon waza* – basic or fundamental techniques.

*kobo-itchi* – the principle that there can be no separation between defence and offence in combat.

*kohai* – an *aikidoka* that is junior to another in rank and/or length of experience in the practice of aikido.

*koho ukemi* – backward rolling 'breakfall'.

*kokyu* – 'breath'.

*kokyu ryoku* – breath power.

*koryu* – ancient (or classical).

*kote gaeshi* – 'wrist turn, outward', where, as a result of turning the wrist, *uke*'s balance is broken to the rear.

*kote hineri* – 'wrist twist, inward', where, as a result of this twisting, *uke*'s balance is broken to the front.

*kyu* – grade awarded to an *aikidoka* below the rank of *shodan* (1st *dan*).

*maai* – combative distance, where space is controlled to deny or gain advantage.

*mae geri* – front kick.

*marui* – circular motion.

*mawashi geri* – side kick.

*metsubushi* – or smashing eye-blow.

*migi* – right.

*migi kamae* – right posture, or stance.

*mokuso* – a period of meditative calm, conducted in *seiza* before and after an aikido class.

*morote dori* – where *nage*'s arm is seized and held by *uke* with two hands.

*mugamae* – 'no-posture'.

*mushin* – 'no-mind'.

*nage* – the defender, and the executor of the decisive technique in an aikido exchange; also *tori* (*Tomiki Aikido*), *sh'te* (*Yoshinkan Aikido*).

*nage waza* – where *uke* is thrown to the ground by *nage*.

*ogi* – 'hidden' techniques; the highest and most subtle level of technical application.

*O Sensei* – 'great teacher', used to describe the founder of aikido, Morihei Ueshiba.

*randori* – 'free' or open practice of techniques; where *tori* (*nage*) spontaneously responds to attacks from *uke* with freely chosen techniques.

*reigi-saho* – forms of etiquette.

*rei-shiki* – or forms of ceremony and etiquette.

*ritsu-rei* – a standing bow.

*ryote dori* – where both *nage*'s hands are seized and held by *uke*.

*ryote dori tenchi nage* – grasped hands heaven and earth throw.

*samurai* – the aristocratic warrior class of pre-Meiji Japan.

*sei ritsu* – natural standing position.

*seishi o choetsu* – transcending thought about life or death.

*seiza* – sitting on the knees folded beneath you.

*sempai* – an aikidoka that is senior to another in rank and/or length of experience in the practice of aikido.

*sensei* – teacher, literally 'born before'.

*shiai* – a contest bout.

*shihonage* -or 'four direction' throw.

*shikko* – walking on the knees.

*shimoseki* – the lower side of the *dojo*.

*shimoza* – the lower seat.

*shin budo* – 'new budo'; martial arts created after the restoration of the Emperor Meiji in the late 19th Century.

*shisei* – posture.

*shizen hontai* – neutral stance of the body (alternatively, *shizentai*).

*shodan* – first dan, the first black belt grade in Japanese (*Shin Budo*) martial arts.

*shomen* – 'head', the wall that serves as the front 'head' or focus of the *dojo*.

*shomen uchi* – a strike with the knife hand, *tegatana*, to the centre of the head.

*shumatsu dosa* – after class exercises, used in *Yoshinkan Aikido*.

*suwari waza* – aikido techniques applied where both *nage* and *uke* are seated in *seiza*.

*tachi waza* – aikido techniques applied where both *nage* and *uke* are standing.

*taigi* – a form of competitive practice, where a number of set techniques are demonstrated within a time limit and marked for performance used in *Shin Shin Toitsu Aikido*.

*tai no henko* – body change movement.

*tai no shintai* – body movement.

*taisabaki* – body positioning to avoid attack and accompanied by a manoeuvre to make an effective counter response.

*taiso* – physical exercises.

*takenomo* – alcove space.

*tanden* – the 'one point' located to 2cm below the navel and said to be the centred point of the body from which *ki* can be located and drawn out.

*tanto* – knife.

*tanto randori shiai* – a 'contest' bout where two players each take it in turn to use and to defend (with aikido technique) against attacks with a rubber 'knife'. Successful striking with the knife or application of aikido technique is awarded points to determine the winner.

*tatami* – mats, the mats covering the *dojo* floor.

*tegatana* – hand-blade.

*tekubi-waza* – or techniques that attack vulnerable points in the wrist joints.

*tenchi nage* – 'heaven and earth throw'.

*tenkan* – is a movement by which *nage*, the defender, pivots away from the incoming path of *uke*'s attack.

*toshu randori shiai* – a 'contest' bout where two players attempt to apply aikido technique against each other freely. Successful application of aikido technique is awarded points to determine the winner.

*tsugi-ashi* – glide walking.

*tsuki* – a punch or thrust to the stomach, chest or face.

*tsukuri* – 'structuring', whereby the skilful use of eye-contact (*metsuke*), posture, hand movements and unbalancing (*kuzushi*), are combined to enable the aikidoka to throw or control an opponent.

*uchi-deshi* – a student who lives with his teacher in a close apprentice to master relationship.

*uke* – the *aikidoka* who takes the fall or receives the control; effectively the 'loser' in a martial encounter.

*ukemi* – 'breakfalls': the art of controlled falling so as not to cause harm to the body.

*ushiro dori* – where *nage* is seized and held from behind by *uke*.

*wa* – harmony.

*waza* – techniques.

*yokomen uchi*, *migi* (right) or *hidari* (left) – a strike with the knife hand, *tegatana*, to the side of the head.

*yoko ukemi* – 'breakfalls' to the side.

*zanshin* – or 'lingering spirit', where *nage* focuses his concentration and 'remaining' posture over his fallen opponent, subduing *uke*'s will to resist further.

*zenpo kaiten* – forward rolling breakfall.

*zarei* – a seated bow.

# USEFUL ADDRESSES

**W**ithin the UK the coaching and ethical standards of aikido organisations are regulated by the British Aikido Board, recognised by the Sports Council as the sole governing body for aikido. The BAB represents over 30 groups and associations, practising a wide variety of styles. Some of these groups are small and may not be officially recognised by the founding organisations of their styles in Japan. If you wish to practice internationally or in Japan, this may be an important consideration when choosing a club.

A BAB affiliated club should guarantee that the instructor has both First Aid and Public Liability Insurance, and that if he or she is a registered Coach, they will have attended and met the requirements of a training programme taught by qualified National Coaching Foundation tutors.

### BRITISH AIKIDO BOARD

*Contact*: Shirley Timms
6 Halkincroft
Langley, Slough
Berks, SL3 7AT
UK

## UK
**British Aikido Federation** (BAB member)
*Contact*: Peter Megann
Yew Tree Cottage
Toot Baldon
Oxon OX9 9NE
(Affiliated to Aikido World Headquarters and a member of the International Aikido Federation and European Aikido Federation).

**UK Aikikai** (BAB member)
*Contact*: Anne Milner
Milestone Cottage
Old Alcester Road
Portway, Nr Birmingham
B48 7NT
(Technical Director: Chiba Sensei
Chief Instructor: Mike Smith 6th Dan
Affiliated to the *Aikikai Hombu*).

## Japan
**Aikido World Headquarters: The Aikikai Hombu**
17–18 Wakamatsu-cho
Shinjuku-ju, Tokyo 154
Tel: 3–3203–9236
Fax: 3–3204–8145

## UK

**British Yoshinkan Aikido Federation: Taidokan Dojo**
(BAB member)
Contact: Anthony Yates
Unit 17, The Lincolnsfield Centre
Bushey Hall Drive
Bushey, Watford
Hertfordshire WD2 2ER
Tel: 0923–817–308

## Japan

**International Yoshinkan Aikido Federation:**
**Yoshinkan Hombu Dojo**
2–28–8 Kami Ochiai
Shinjuku-ku, Tokyo 161
Tel: 3–3368–5556
Fax: 81–3–3368–5578

## TOMIKI AIKIDO

## UK

**British Aikido Association** (BAB member)
*Contact*: The BAA Registrar
'Sunrise'
The Hatch
Burghfield Village
Reading, Berks RG3 3TJ
(President: Bill Lawrence 7th Dan).

## Japan

**All Japan Aikido Association** and the
**Tomiki Aikido International Network**
*Contact*: Itsuo Haba
International Division
Shakujiidai 6–15–18–701
Nerima-ku, Tokyo 177

### KI AIKIDO

## UK

**Ki Society of the UK** (BAB member)
5 Hopkins Road
Counden, Coventry
CV6 1BD

## Japan

**Ki Society World Headquarters/Ki No Sato**
**Ki no Kenkyukai So-Honbu**
3515 O-aza Akabane
Ichikai-machi
Haga-gun
Tochiga-ken
Tel: 0285–68–4000

# PRINCIPLES OF ACUPUNCTURE

## ANGELA HICKS

Acupuncture is a Chinese therapy whose efficacy is well known in the Western medical community. It has been proved effective in treating a wide range of conditions, from asthma to high blood pressure. This book provides anyone contemplating treatment a useful overview of acupuncture and the principles of Chinese medicine including:

- how diagnosis is made in Chinese medicine
- which illnesses acupuncture treats effectively
- how the needles are used and how they affect your body systems
- how to find a practitioner.

Angela Hicks is joint-principal of the College of Integrated Chinese Medicine in Reading, England, where she also teaches and is a clinical supervisor. She has practised acupuncture for over 20 years and is the author of *Principles of Chinese Medicine*.

# PRINCIPLES OF TAI CHI

PAUL BRECHER

In an inspiring and informative style, this comprehensive introduction to Tai Chi includes a discussion of all the main Tai Chi styles rather than focusing on one specific tradition. The guide explains:

- what Tai Chi is
- how to use Tai Chi techniques for health and healing
- the best way to train in Tai Chi.

Paul Brecher has been practising martial arts for over twenty years. He is an Instructor for the World Tai Chi Boxing Association and has demonstrated Tai Chi on television. He is also a qualified practitioner of Acupuncture and Traditional Chinese Herbal Medicine.

# PRINCIPLES OF SELF-HEALING

## DAVID LAWSON

In these high pressure times we are in need of ways of relaxing and gaining a sense of happiness and peace. There are many skills and techniques that we can master to bring healing and well-being to our minds and bodies.

This introductory guide includes:

- visualizations to encourage our natural healing process
- affirmations to guide and inspire
- ways of developing the latent power of the mind
- techniques for gaining a deeper understanding of yourself and others

David Lawson is a teacher, healer and writer. He has worked extensively with Louise Hay, author of *You Can Heal Your Life*, and runs workshops throughout the world. He is the author of several books on the subject, including *I See Myself in Perfect Health*, also published by Thorsons.

# PRINCIPLES OF YOGA

## CHERYL ISAACSON

Yoga is a time-honoured system of balancing mind, body and spirit. Originally part of the mystical wisdom of Indian philosophy, Western cultures have mostly emphasized its physical practices. These are, however, only one aspect of the integrated way of life which yoga provides. This introduction explains:

- how yoga postures fit into the total yoga system
- ways to use yoga thought and action in daily life
- simple methods for relaxing and meditating
- how to take charge of your own health and energy
- the secrets of personal peace and stability

Cheryl Isaacson is an experienced yoga practitioner and teacher. She is also a journalist specializing in health, fitness and alternative medicine. Her book *Yoga: Step by Step* is published by Thorsons. She takes an active interest in studying spiritual and mystical traditions worldwide.

# PRINCIPLES OF REIKI

## KAJSA KRISHNI BORANG

A comprehensive introduction to the Japanese healing system that is growing rapidly in popularity. This introduction explains:

- what Reiki is
- the different Reiki lineages and initiation processes
- what to expect from a Reiki treatment
- where to find a Reiki practitioner

Kajsa Krishni Borang has been a Reiki master since 1984. She has taught Reiki internationally. Kasja lived in Swami Muktananda's ashram for six years and was initiated into the lineage by Vanja Twam. She is now based in the UK, where she runs regular workshops.

# PRINCIPLES OF BUDDHISM

KULANANDA

More and more people are turning towards Buddhism, disillusioned by the materialism of our times and attracted by the beauty and simplicity of this way of life. This introductory guide describes the growth of modern Buddhism and explains:

- who the Buddha was
- the ideas and beliefs at the heart of Buddhism
- how to meditate
- the main types of Buddhism in the world today

Kulananda has worked within the Friends of the Western Buddhist Order since 1975. Ordained in 1977, he is now a leading member of the Western Buddhist Order and, as a teacher, writer, speaker and organizer, is devoted to creating contexts in which Westerners can practise Buddhism.

# PRINCIPLES OF SHIATSU

CHRIS JARMEY

Shiatsu is an Eastern therapeutic technique which uses pressure to enhance the flow of life energy - or ki - within the body. This introductory guide is ideal for the beginner or student of this increasingly popular therapy, and for anyone with a serious interest in bodywork. In this accessible and informative book, experienced shiatsu practitioner Chris Jarmey explains the concept of ki, the power which unifies and animates the channels as they are used in shiatsu, the basic treatment techniques and how shiatsu can help specific ailments.